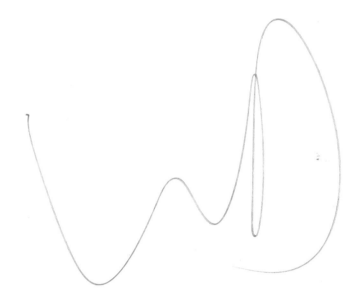

CONTEMPORARY JEWELRY DESIGN

Liu Xiao, Li Puman
Academic Advisor_Jivan Astfalck

CYPI PRESS

CONTENTS

1 CONVERSATION WITH TRADITION

2 EYES ON EVERYDAY LIFE

MEDITATION ON SELF

QUESTION BASED ON EXPLORATION

CONTEMPORARY JEWELRY
Foreword | **DESIGN**

Despite its short history, contemporary jewelry art has demonstrated extraordinarily abundant and diverse features. With its original identity continuously changing and its edges extending and overlapping with history, society, and cultural arts, jewelry has become a featured contemporary art topic. Using jewelry as a medium of expression, jewelry artists have delved into constant exploration and practice from various aspects, such as materials, methods, craftsmanship, and concepts. Some artists even take on more extensive artistic creation of jewelry based on artistic discussions and research of social and cultural phenomena. All of their works center on jewelry design with a focus on interacting with the viewers and the society at large in vivid and various ways.

Contemporary jewelry art has become a common topic in the global context. This book makes every effort to cover different countries and areas across the globe in terms of artists, which gives a comparatively comprehensive display of the styles of creators from various areas. More importantly, the rich demonstration of these styles takes the reader further to, among others, the origins, features, and diversity of the artworks. There are both widely accepted artworks in this book and also some deeper, more conceptual and experimental artistic forays. Some of them may not be so brilliant in appearance, yet embrace extremely precious concepts and philosophies. This book, demonstrating the creation processes and splendid examples of contemporary jewelry artists who have a niche on the international stage, probes the interrelation between jewelry arts and the society from a more macroscopic perspective. Editors of this book exerted themselves to give full expression to all the works, artistic concepts, inspiration origins, design drafts, and composition processes of the artists and artistic experiments derived from them. The abundant unusual, one-of-a-kind contemporary jewelry artworks in the book serve as reflection of various shapes and features of the world in their small and tiny forms.

I would like to extend my gratitude particularly to Professor Jivan Astfalck, the renowned German Jewelry artist and educationist, and Professor Teng Fei who is recognized as "the pioneer of China's art jewelry." Their contribution to this book has opened our eyes not only to abundant visual artworks with a diverse and multi-faceted record of the creative process, but also to discussions and meditations engendered by contemporary jewelry development.

Liu Xiao

March 2014, Beijing

CONTEMPORARY JEWELRY
Preface | **DESIGN**

Whose jewelry is it anyway?

Jivan Astfalck

Jewelry artist, educationist

End of 2013

Whose jewelry is it anyway?

Reinventing "contemporary" studio jewelry in a global world

Thinking Materials-Forming Ideas

The debate about the impact of crafts practice and studio jewelry in particular, its relevance and positioning in the wider discourse of contemporary art is interesting, both if considered as a mode of cultural production, and also as a subject-specific discipline with its own histories, parameters and challenges. I am interested in these issues not only as an educator and theorist, but also as a visual artist who works conceptually through craft. My theoretical approach is informed by methods of artistic practice and pedagogies, which emphasize polyphonic thinking, and aim to strengthen engagements with notions of ambivalence and dialogical dynamics. In my view, such an emphasis is necessary because methodologies for disseminating historical material need to be developed, which are flexible enough to account for co-existing histories (there never exists only one history alone) and also to develop artistic jewelry practice from within diverse cultures of jewelry making. This is especially true as we are increasingly within a global culture of shared values and beliefs.

In a world of increasingly internationalised information sharing, educational and economic migration, many aspects of distinction and difference are disappearing: We dress in similar ways, sit on the same plastic chairs wherever we travel and encounter the same brands across the world. The students who are working with me (and others, too, of course) bring their study experience back to their countries; gradually we see similar cultures of making and studio practice methodologies appearing across the globe. Young and aspiring jewelry artists, designers, and makers across the world find themselves taught in similar ways, confronted with similar conceptual design values, and a shared information system.

To forestall a lack of original design enquiries and conformity within the subject area (and this applies, in my view, to all creative subjects) there is a distinct need for creative space that allows for exploratory methods of individualised design development and authentic experience, which in turn must be underpinned by theoretical and critical methods that are flexible enough to engage with polyphonic creative disciplines. When I say "polyphonic," imagine a choir, which might consist of hundreds of highly individual voices, but together they make a perfect sound.

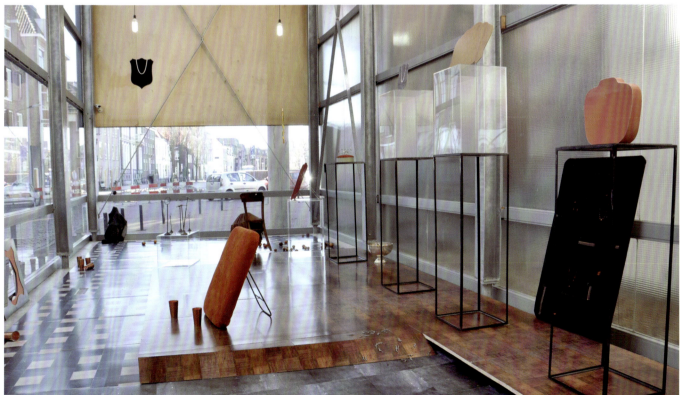

The abandonment of a carefully constructed cultural identity becomes identity itself as much as making become porous, counterhistorical and hybrid.

1 | 2
—————
3 | 4

1 Iris Eichenberg, Pink Years Later, Brooch
2 Benjamin Lignel, Suppléments, Brooch
3 Heejoo Kim, Fifth Season, Brooch
4 Shen Yi, Ourselves Beside Me, Necklace

In our contemporary culture, we might regard any attempt to re-connect to a personal or cultural point of origin as nostalgic; we find ourselves much more in a world of shifting, flexible frameworks in which our origins, bonds, traditions, our sentiments and dreams, exist alongside other stories, other fragments of memory and traces of time. In such a world a creative practitioner is a voyager, a person on a journey wandering, or, more likely, meandering through the world of appearances, ideas, images, theories and histories. The abandonment of a carefully constructed cultural identity becomes identity itself, as much as making becomes porous, counter-historical and hybrid. On the other side of the spectrum we find utopian ideals, the hope for a "better" world, and the passionate investment in the idea that objects have embedded meaning and "have" therefore the power to contribute to the achievement of such ideals.

We find crafts objects of un-definable origin on sale everywhere, permeating crafts markets, mail order catalogues, department stores, and fashion and gifts shops. Even in the face of the pressure to desire only what others already possess and thus to succumb to what Jean Baudrillard has termed a culture of profound monotony[1] we want to distinguish ourselves as individuals. One way to attempt this is through the acquisition of objects, which via their symbolic assimilation mark us as individuals. Consumption is in this respect not only understood as acquisition, but as expression as well. What is experienced as the expression of individualism is individualism

[1] Baudrillard, Jean "The System of Objects" in *Jean Baudrillard: Selected Writings, Poster, Mark (ed.)*, Oxford: Polity Press, 1988

only as long as the patterns of consumption respond to the aspirations of the group and can be recognised as such.

It is suggested that in an idealist-consumerist society, personalised relationships with objects substitute the actual lived and conflict-inherent human relations – and in particular, with objects that sit close to, onto, or in the body. There exists, however, an interesting dichotomy between the designed commodity on the one hand and conceptually-focused creative work. Concept-focused work can be explored in a much looser relationship to commodity and culture. This work relates uniquely to art history – it is the result of a creative practice that references its own visual and conceptual history and can exist outside the dynamics of trading and monetary exchange. Most studio jewellers whose studio practice I am familiar with, engage with the tension between the functionality of the object, its status as a consumer good, and a more ideas-based artistic agenda, all at the same time; hence much of the confusion about how to classify artistic practice into design-led, crafts-based, or art-practice. This is never a simple equation, and it gets even more complicated and indeed interesting, when jewellers use the visual appearance of banal popular culture, kitsch, the ephemeral of every-day life and/or degraded materials with which they re-create the tired and clichéd object as an object filled with fresh questioning and visual resonance.

We practice, learn and teach, exhibit and sell, in a market situation where crafts, art and design have to simulate their own already established visual, material and conceptual identities to be economically successful. Every maker who has not quite made it into the realm of economic self-sufficiency knows how hard it is to sell objects, which remain outside of the standard territory of commodity significance, and to achieve artistic autonomy. And every maker, who has made that leap successfully knows, or should know, that the particularities of their artistic production, the recognisable marketable style, is what they sell – and how much work it took to get there in the first place, presumably with a lot of sacrifices on the way. Market identities and name branding possibly always existed in the art world, but were eschewed as toxic values which undermined the transcendent value of art. We only need to look at the rise of the mega-art fair (Basel, Frieze, etc.) to realise that things have changed. I recently watched "Harry Potter" viewing a butterfly painting by Damien Hirst (at "Frieze" in London), an uncanny experience that left me unsure on which level of reality I was operating. Some people believe that only when a piece of art has been "christened" by the art market, when it has been sold and ideally re-sold, is it art, elevating the economic value of a piece of creative work beyond other possible and co-existing values (apart from the fact that money appears to be regarded as transcendent

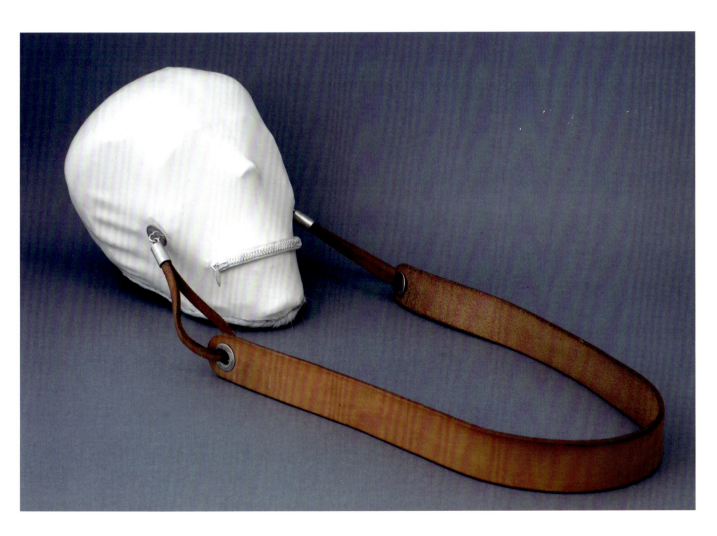

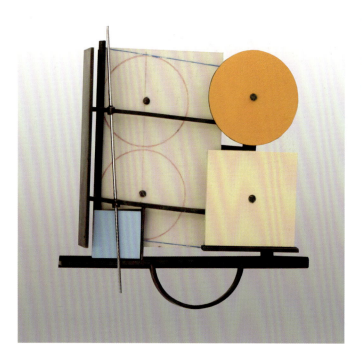

value here… but that is another essay). This is not only an economic issue, but very much a political one, too.

The way creative production is supported in any given country very much determines its infrastructure. How is the development of a gallery system in a country supported? How is access to distribution opportunities further away than one's hometown facilitated, what grants, bursaries and mentoring systems exist to bridge the crucial gap between studio and audience? In Britain, for example, we do not have a supported gallery system for craft, and for jewelry art in particular, the situation in this respect is dire, but other systems have developed which seem to fill the gap to some extent. Opportunities for artist residencies, socially motivated art projects, community support projects, collaborative funded projects, etc. are vibrant and inclusive. Many of these projects are self-initiated and are developed with the aim to become self-sufficient; for example, already established arts professional collectives, like Craftspace in Birmingham, have created others. Craftspace is an arts organisation that develops both the artists and the audience; their objectives address issues around the role and value of contemporary crafts, including skill, access, identity, aesthetics of difference, exploration of ideas and the changing nature of crafts practice in relation to other art forms.[2] Craftspace serves as an example for the kind of professional organisation, which I believe is vital for the future of studio crafts practice. Empathetic to the artists' enquires and their specific needs to develop, they are interested in cultural dissemination, view artmaking as a relevant reflective language, and

they are sensitive to the contribution crafts make to the community and wellbeing. In working relationships with organisations like these, makers can resist becoming the makers of their own brand and can afford to remain creatively inquisitive and evolving.

We need to break with the traditional passive attitudes in our understanding of the viability of the craft object and make sustainability of inquisitive studio practice a priority. This requires a fundamental shift in the learning and teaching methodologies with which we enable young practitioners. In the many years I have been teaching, I have witnessed, and contributed to, the shift from skills-based learning to design-development-focused crafts practice. But now I believe we are in the midst of another shift, where some crafts practices provide a counter-position and resistance to the homogenisation of the global commodity market and, at times, can offer meaningful conceptual depth.

And this is why we need to look again at what distinguishes a craft-based design practice from a craft-based art practice, and how the two modes of enquiry and representation relate to each other.

Jewelry artists use their practice as a way of challenging stereotypical and clichéd representations, including those of relationships, gender, and body. They use subtle and intelligent provocation to draw attention to conventions of seeing, which can be resisted and re-invested; what is perceived as problematic can be re-imagined and reconfigured in the creative process. This dynamic in particular has engendered a vibrant creative

[2] http://www.craftspace.co.uk

culture where the status of the object is investigated in relation to the cultured body. It has created a jewelry-making culture where the primary function of every-day wearability is not regarded as primary, but has been replaced by subject-specific representational techniques and enquiries. So much so, that at one end of the scale a whole set of presentation strategies which exist outside the object itself have been added to the available vocabulary and are, it seems at times, endlessly repeated by too many practitioners – the display furniture of art jewelry. It raises the question of the status of the object anew and with some urgency. How is an object developed where the conceptual enquiry is embedded and not added-on?

The re-description the artist mediates in his or her jewelry work is guided by the interplay between difference and resemblance. Studio jewellers of this kind create work out of an existing crafts "vocabulary" and in doing so create new meaning and objects with re-invested emotive value. The objects offer a counter-position to common notions of the beautiful by infiltrating the wearable decorative objects with unexpected details, surprising choices of materials, and/or a twist in the meaning of the work to keep any metaphorical charge alive (in contrast to a "dead" metaphor). It is from this tensive apprehension that a new vision springs forth, one which ordinary vision resists because it is attached to the ordinary use of forms and signs, including those of "dead" metaphors. The eclipse of the objective, established and therefore increasingly

meaningless, thus makes way for the revelation of a new dimension of reality and truth, subjective as this might be.

Aesthetic experience, in my view, is constituted within the hermeneutic continuity of human existence and can therefore only be appropriately discussed in this wider framework.[3]

The term hermeneutics is usually understood as the study of the theory and practice of interpretation, but covers both the first order art and the second order theory of understanding and interpretation of linguistic and non-linguistic expressions.

I would like to come back to what I said earlier about the need for differentiation between design and art in the global market, and how we need to address education differently to prepare for this emerging world. When we take a step sideways and use a hermeneutic approach, categories like craft, design, art, and I'd like to add, fashion, are rendered useless, because aesthetic experience is characterised as intuition, indeed as a world-view, Weltanschauung – literally an intuition of the world. This does not simply mean that creative practice justifies its own claim to truth over and against other types of knowledge, insofar as the free play of the imagination tends towards "knowledge in general". It also means that the "inner intuition" in play brings the world, and not just the objects in it, to intuition[4] – and in doing so we are creating culture together!

This is an image (image 4, page XIII) of my twenty-seven 2013 MA students, many from Asian backgrounds. They are photographed here mapping out their reference points between fashion, art, craft and design, their aims and objectives and their life-aspirations. When externalised and made visual like this, it creates a complicated picture, but not at all a confounding one – it shows that creating

a simplistic or clichéd handle on this complexity would seriously impinge on creative possibilities and the richness with which we can create. It also shows that we can create together without loosing our identities and differences and that by doing so we find many crossover points, full of potential for dialogue and collaboration.

If we take the four cardinal points: fashion, art, craft and design and use them for orientation in terms of positioning practice methodologies, historical reference and applied technologies, we could use these points like a stellar system or any other navigation tool to find our audiences, and my feeling is that we would have much better journeys!

Palimpsests and other forms of mash-ups, where references are deconstructed, re-constructed, used with irony or without, often used with counter-historical and/or cross-cultural intentions, stand in stark contrast to Modernism's ideal of the purified form, the autonomous object and in socio-political terms notions of national cultural identity. They allow forms of the past to emerge and to coexist, sometimes as fragments or ruins, like in much contemporary jewelry which up-cycles and/or uses found objects, alongside a riot of other references, including those of modernism, while searching for a new and authentic sense of identity, meaning, and belonging.

Jewelry artists, and some design practitioners, work with a shared visual and methodological vocabulary in addition to the visual vocabulary, which comes with a particular cultural belonging and/or upbringing. The subject discipline is mature, reflective, and informed enough to reference a shared system of value and interpretation. It is vital, therefore, that individualised artistic practice and creative exploration continues to react against a culture in which the

[3] Gadamer, H.G. (1960: 169–171) *Aesthetic and Hermeneutical Implications: Reconstruction and Integration as Hermeneutical Tasks, in Truth and Method*, Tübingen: Niemeyer

[4] Gadamer, H.G. (1986: 164) *Appendix: Intuition and Vividness, in the Relevance of the Beautiful and Other Essays*, Cambridge: Cambridge University Press

<table>
<tr><td></td><td>2</td></tr>
<tr><td>1</td><td>3</td></tr>
<tr><td></td><td>4</td></tr>
</table>

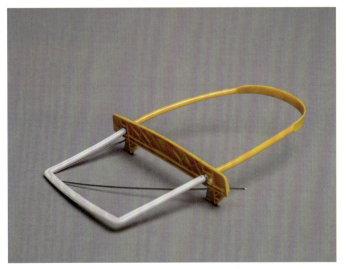

generation of unlimited series of variables, like the made-to-measure or the hand-made with its idiosyncratic markings, has been replaced by production of a limited number of constants, which creates that aspect of global culture, which is of such unprecedented boredom. The focus on the every-day, the domestic, the hand-made and idiosyncratic, the marginalized and excluded, which can be observed in so much contemporary jewelry, seems to be a direct reflection on a continuously more homogenous world culture, where difference and individuality come at an increasingly high price. So much more important are working methodologies that intelligently enable the reconstruction of signs and their creative and social function and allow for making as an authentic experience.

These artistic methodologies differ from a "classical" design process, based on function and form, insofar as they take their impetus from an awareness of the world, question established values and visual appearances – more often than not actually bridging two (or more) concurrent value systems. Alongside the acquisition of skills and thoughtful handling of ideas, tomorrow's generation of artists and designers will need to have sensitivity and knowledge of cultural issues, confidence in using idea-based strategies, and a much deeper knowledge of professional practice and cross-cultural communication opportunities. They will engage with questions of how inherited beliefs shift when exposed to different ones, how new perspectives emerge when exposed to different ways of knowing and learning, and if this can create new communities of shared values – values which inform our making cultures, negotiate and mediate the boundaries of creative disciplines without loosing subject-specific and already established knowledge, and make "making" relevant in a shared global world.

1

CONVERSATION WITH TRADITION

The jewelry artists draw their inspiration from meditation on traditional art and culture. Inquiry, inheritance, and development of the tradition are the significant features of the transition that contemporary jewelry art assumes.

Ramon Puig Cuyàs

The word "jewelry" in Catalan, "joia," also means, "sharing." Ramon believes the processes of design and creating are emotional experiences with multiple meaningful moments. In his search for combinations and possibilities, Ramon constantly forages for the unknown and creates contrasts with previous draft models to uncover new chances of reorganization; this insures that all the details and elements are interrelated with each other as a unified whole. During this process, Ramon hopes that his joyous experiences can be imparted to the wearers so as to sublimate the jewels to become spiritual symbols.

The series of "Net-Works," an epitome of the boundless universe with no two identical elements, tries to locate an optimal state between straight lines and curved lines with few colors. Ramon expects his works to boast the ability to create a universal order symbolizing the abstract, and establish a kind of equilibrium between the microscopic and macroscopic domains around us. Meanwhile, he wishes to represent in his finished works the dialectical relationship between order and chaos.

1 | 2

1 Net-Works Series – 1
Brooch, 2011
Oxidized nickel, silver
90×55×12 mm
Photography: Ramon Puig Cuyàs

2 Net-Works Series – 2
Brooch, 2011
Oxidized nickel, silver
80×70×15 mm
Photography: Ramon Puig Cuyàs

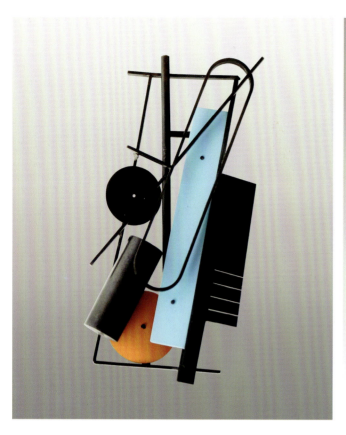

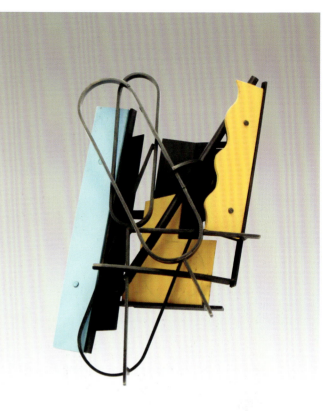

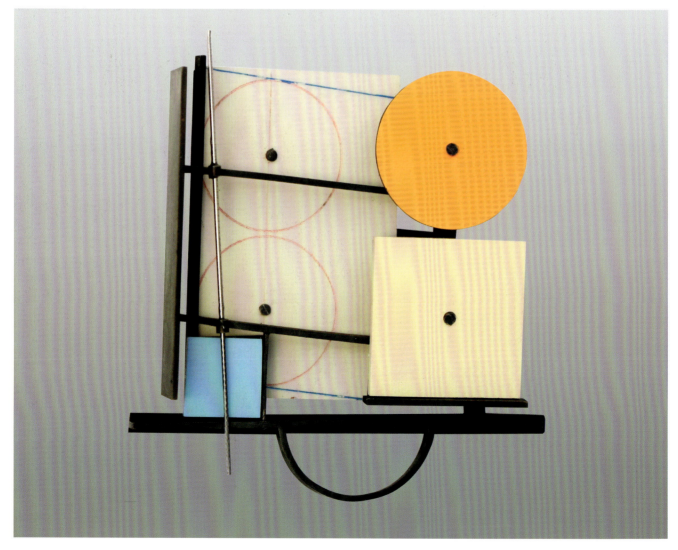

1 Subtle Architectures Series – 9
Brooch, 2012
Oxidized nickel, silver
95×45×20 mm
Photography: Ramon Puig Cuyàs

2 Subtle Architectures Series – 10
Brooch, 2013
Oxidized nickel, silver,
55×60×12 mm
Photography: Ramon Puig Cuyàs

3 The artist's worktable

4 Sketches of the "Subtle
Architectures Series"

2011   mº 1382

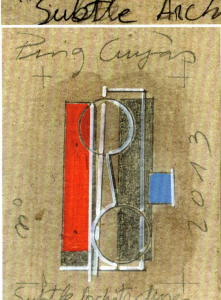

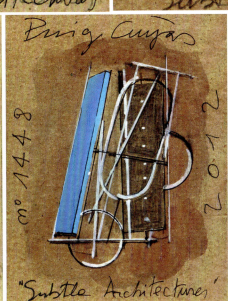

Kazumi Nagano

Kazumi Nagano majored in Japanese-style painting at university and graduate school, and was once a Japanese-style painter. This training still influences her present work.

Her artistic concept is to produce "calm and beautiful" work because she thinks that the essence of Japanese culture is calm and beautiful. She would like to make work that is not simply a copy of the western styles. She wishes people to feel an internal Japanese spirit instead of a superficial one. Kazumi makes a sheet with the handloom and folds it into three-dimensional jewelry using the Japanese traditional technique of origami. It is the most suitable way of production. Folding a sheet requires only her feelings for any material, such as gold, Japanese paper, or bamboo tape.

1 Untitled – 1
Brooch, 2009
Japanese paper, 18 kt gold,
Pin– 950 silver, nylon thread, Japanese lacquer
95×95×53 mm
Photography: Mitsuo Shimada

2-3 Untitled – 2
Brooch, 2013
Bamboo Tape, Nylon Thread,
18 kt gold, mino–Japanese paper tape, Pin– 950 silver
125×80×55 mm (left),
110×120×60 mm (right)
Photography: Ryota Seloguchi

4 Untitled – 3
Brooch, 2013
Bamboo tape, nylon thread, 18 kt gold,
Pin– 950 silver
125×90×40 mm
Photography: Ryota Seloguchi

5 Untitled – 4
Brooch, 2013
Bamboo tape, nylon thread, 18 kt gold,
Pin– 950 Silver
120×110×50 mm
Photography: Ryota Seloguchi

1 | 2   **1** Untitled – 5
Bracelet, 2010
Gold (18, 14, 10 kt), nylon thread
Diameter: 70 mm; height: 60 mm
Photography: Mitsuo Shimada

2 Untitled – 6
Brooch, 2010
Platinum 900, 18 kt gold, nylon thread,
diamond beads, Pin- 950 silver
70×65×55 mm
Photography: Mitsuo Shimada

Evert Nijland

Evert Nijland's jewelry is based on images and themes out of Western art history. In his work, he does research on the dialogue between the past and the present by interpreting and translating the historical material into his own contemporary context. Evert's work is not about nostalgia for the past, but about archetypes and themes that are relevant even today.

Evert's designs draw from visual elements of works, for example, by da Vinci and Lucas Cranach, and interact closely with artistic styles in the 18th century. Evert is keen on designing necklaces and brooches. He holds that brooches can ideally pose challenges of making an elevated structure, which prompts

1 | 2
3

1 "Nocturne," from "Ornament" series
Brooch, 2012
Wood, glass, steel silver
Height: 90 mm
Photography: Eddo Hartmann

2 "Chains," from "Ornament" series
Brooch, 2012
Wood, glass, silver, steel
Height: 90 mm
Photography: Eddo Hartmann

3 "Flowers 2," from "Ornament" series
Brooch, 2012
Wood, glass, silver, steel
Height: 100 mm
Photography: Eddo Hartmann

4 | 5
6 | 7

4 "Piranesi 1," from "Ornament" series
Brooch, 2012
Wood, silver, steel
Height: 120 mm
Photography: Eddo Hartmann

5 "Adadio 2," from "Ornament" series
Brooch , 2012
Wood, glass, hair, steel, textile
Height: 90 mm
Photography: Eddo Hartmann

6 "Piranesi 2," from "Ornament" series
Brooch, 2012
Wood, glass, hair, silver, steel
Height: 120 mm
Photography: Eddo Hartmann

7 "Piranesi 2," from "Ornament" series - back
Brooch, 2012
Digital etching in steel, silver
Height: 120 mm
Photography: Eddo Hartmann

him to clarify the contrast between the general solemn outlines and liberal forms, and to contemplate the "publicity" of the face and the "invisibility" of the back of the brooch. Moreover, such contrasts can be satisfyingly achieved through the selection and application of materials; for instance, by juxtaposition of shabby ancient wood with exquisite glassblowing artwork and combination of plain riveting or binding with refined laser cutting or industrial etching technologies.

1-2 "Pompei 1," from "Ornament"
series
-details

3 "Pompei 1," from "Ornament"
series
Necklace, 2009
Glass, textile, silver
Diameter: 180 mm
Photography: Eddo Hartmann

4 "Pompei 1," from "Ornament"
series
-sketches

5 "Carneool," from "Ornament"
series
Necklace, 2009
Glass, gemstone, textile, silver
Diameter: 180 mm
Photography: Eddo Hartmann

6 "Pompei 2," from "Ornament"
series
Necklace, 2009
Glass, silver, textile
Diameter: 180 mm
Photography: Eddo Hartmann

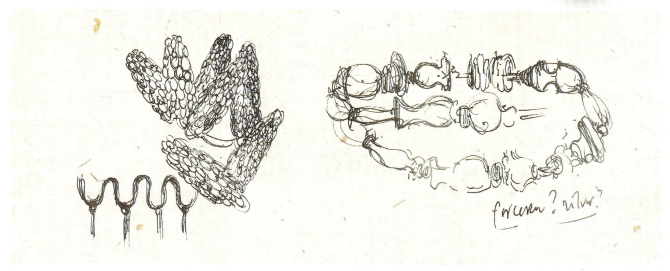

Gigi Mariani

Gigi Mariani has been a goldsmith for over twenty-five years in Modena, Italy. Since he was a young man, he has been interested and attracted to metals and their infinite capabilities, especially overlapping, oxidation, and sequences of layers. With his work, Gigi tries to transfer everyday emotions into contemporary jewelry; he creates unique pieces in a simple, informal and spontaneous way. This permits him to develop new situations, and the art appreciators to develop feelings from these situations. His goal is to move from the concept of simple jewelry, to a larger concept of sculpture and art pieces.

Gigi utilizes antique and unique goldsmith techniques, such as niello and granulation, personalizing them in order to distinguish his work from others'. He works with precious metals, combining them with other metals such as iron, copper, and brass. His jewelry is usually finished by texturing the material, which hides the precious metals to the naked eye. As painters use their canvas to express feelings, Gigi uses his jewelry as a base for expressing his.

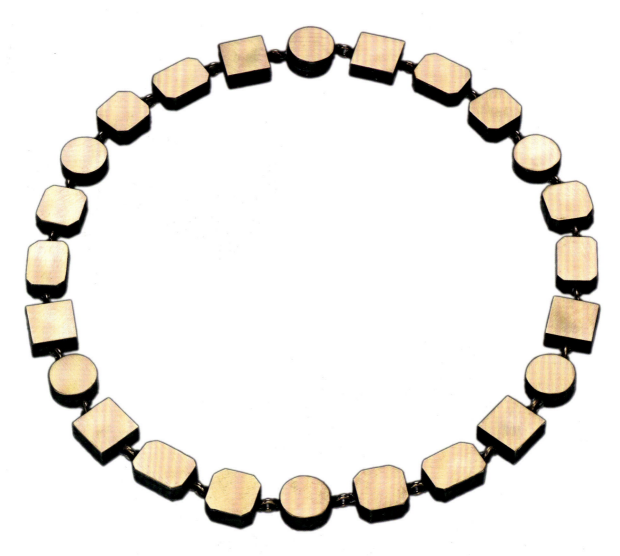

1 Solitaire
Necklace, 2013
Silver, 18 kt red gold, niello, patina

2 Mirrors
Bracelet, 2013
Silver, 18 kt red gold, niello, patina
Diameter: 106 mm; width: 29 mm

3 It's all under control
Bracelet, 2013
Silver, 18 kt yellow gold, niello, patina
Diameter: 105 mm; width: 33 mm

4 Stonehenge
Bracelet, 2012
Silver, 18 kt yellow gold, niello, patina
Diameter: 190 mm; height: 29 mm

1 **1** Rusts
Ring, 2010
Silver, oxidations, patina
45×63×43 mm

2 **2** Track
Ring, 2011
Silver, 18 kt yellow gold, niello,
oxidations, patina
40×60 mm

3 **3** In the signs will remain the memory
Brooch, 2013
Silver, 18 kt yellow gold, niello, patina
75×35×16 mm

Li Puman

Li Puman draws her inspiration from ancient Chinese poetry featuring homesickness. Endowed with succinct diction, distinct rhythms, and harmonious rhymes, ancient Chinese poems manage to express human thoughts and feelings in an accurate and straightforward manner. Nowadays jewelry has also started its evolutionary journey from plain body ornaments to works of art, conveying the most delicate and sincere feelings and thoughts of humankind. Therefore, during Li's design, her infusion of poetry into her jewelry is not only an expression of inner emotions, but also a demonstration of the "poetic attribute" of contemporary jewelry.

1	2	
	3	4

1 "Teardrops on a Flower," from "Returning Home in a Mourning Dream" series
Headdress, 2010
Silver, copper, enamel
70×250×60 mm

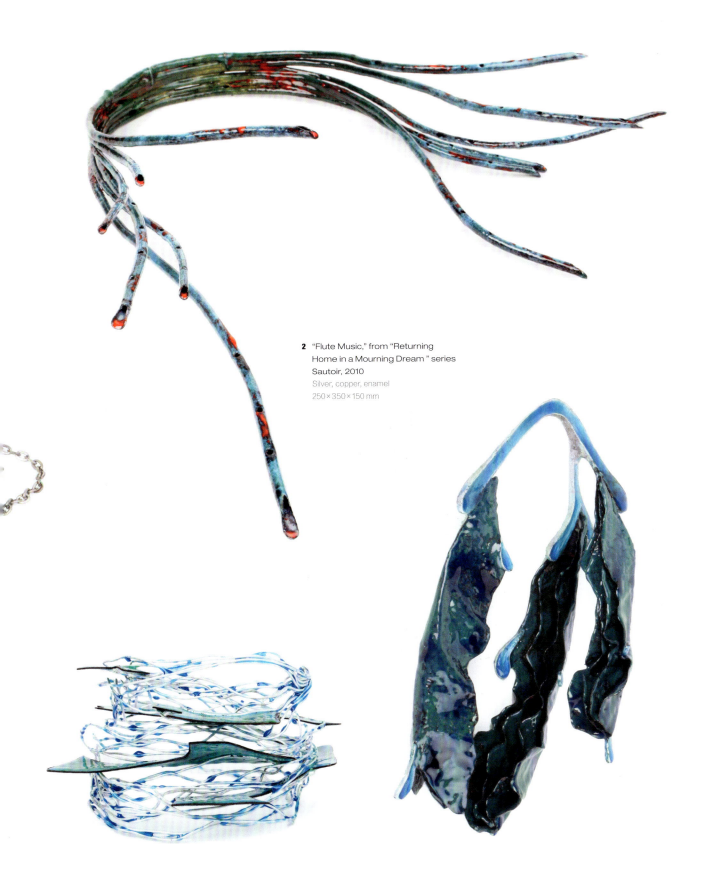

2 "Flute Music," from "Returning
Home in a Mourning Dream" series
Sautoir, 2010
Silver, copper, enamel
250×350×150 mm

3 "Farewell to Home," from "Returning Home
in a Mourning Dream" series
Sautoir, 2010
Silver, copper, enamel
100×90×80 mm

4 "Rain Dripping from Leaves," from
"Returning Home in a Mourning
Dream" series
Earrings, 2010
Silver, copper, enamel
130×60×80 mm

1 "Ten Sights," from "Returning
  Home in a Mourning Dream" series
  Ring, 2010
  Silver, copper, enamel
  30×40×20 mm

2 "Nostalgic Yearning when Leaning
  against Railings," from "Returning Home in a
  Mourning Dream" series
  Ring, 2010
  Silver, copper, enamel
  110×270×30 mm

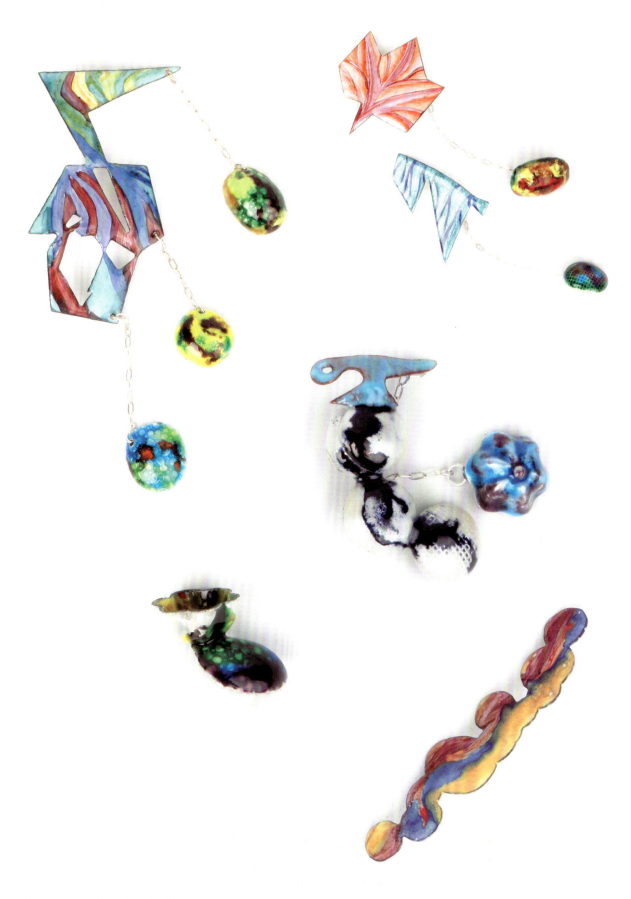

3 "Imprint on the Heart," from "Returning Home in
a Mourning Dream" series
Brooch, 2010
Silver, copper, enamel
60×30×50×20 mm

Yan Manjiang

Yan Manjiang mainly employs the lyrical style of emotional expression in forming objects. She chooses various materials and techniques, such as resin and metal working, to create objects with concepts and artistic values. Her inspiration comes from human instincts and people's feelings upon the first touch of an object. She feels that an object is what people think of it at first glance. Her work, "Lyrics by Objects," based on the symbolism of the peach in China's traditional folk culture, tries to link contemporary urban living with common forms of "peaches and similar emotions" such as "peach blossoms," "peach wood charms," "longevity peaches," "escape" (the Chinese character meaning "escape" is the homonym of the one meaning "peach"), and "a utopian retreat of peace and happiness featuring peach trees." These combinations restore the vitality of traditional symbols and represent the emotional relationships between jewelry and people.

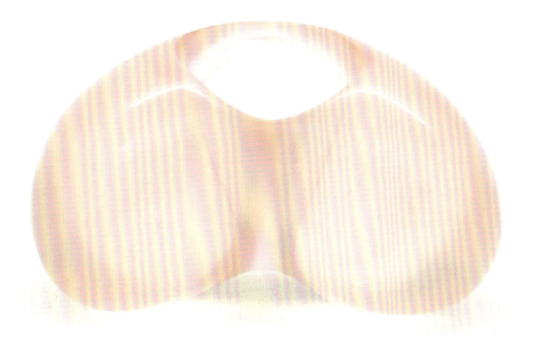

1
—
2

1 Lyrics by Objects – 1
Ring, 2012
Resin, color paste
80×80 mm
2 Lyrics by Objects – 2
Ring, 2012
Resin, color paste
60×60 mm

Zhang Fan

Influenced by the court workmanship and culture of the Ming and Qing Dynasties in China's history, Zhang Fan draws most of her design inspiration from the artistic atmosphere permeating China's classic gardens and poems. She expects her jewelry to possess the dynamic beauty of people dancing to the wind. Therefore, she combines refined metal workman's techniques with modern fabrication processing methods, and applies these to loose and liberal structures. Jewelry fashioned in this way can re-form and change its shape in accordance with the wearer's movements.

1 Evolvement – 1
Sautoir, 2012
Red copper, gilt pure silver, pure gold,
pearl, tourmaline, emerald
650×550×120 mm

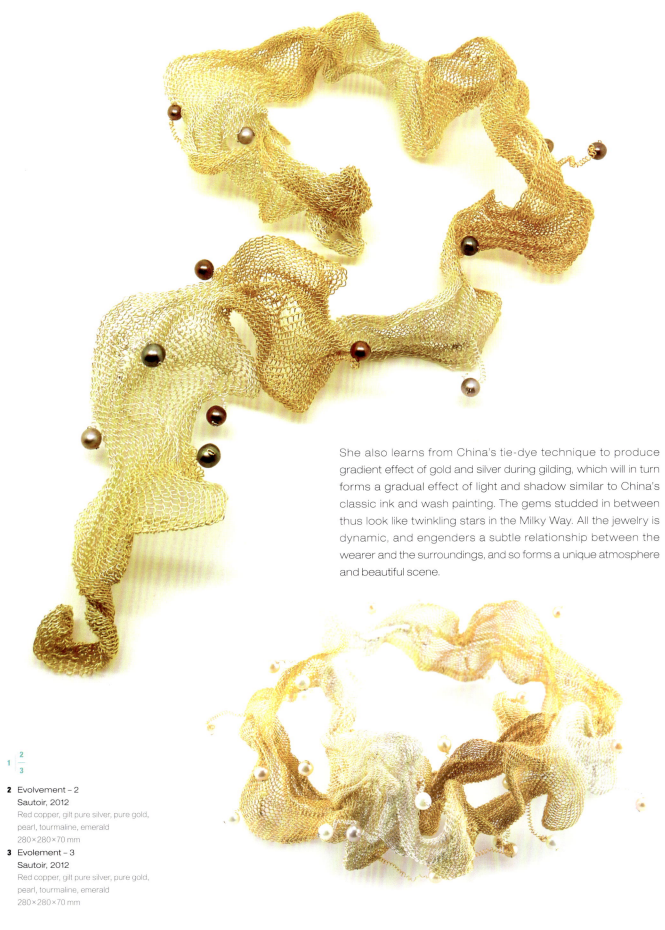

She also learns from China's tie-dye technique to produce gradient effect of gold and silver during gilding, which will in turn forms a gradual effect of light and shadow similar to China's classic ink and wash painting. The gems studded in between thus look like twinkling stars in the Milky Way. All the jewelry is dynamic, and engenders a subtle relationship between the wearer and the surroundings, and so forms a unique atmosphere and beautiful scene.

1 | 2
  | 3

2 Evolvement – 2
Sautoir, 2012
Red copper, gilt pure silver, pure gold,
pearl, tourmaline, emerald
280×280×70 mm

3 Evolement – 3
Sautoir, 2012
Red copper, gilt pure silver, pure gold,
pearl, tourmaline, emerald
280×280×70 mm

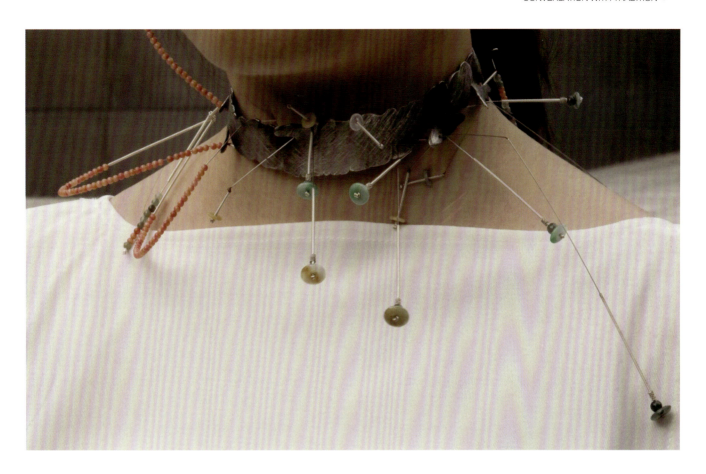

2

EYES ON EVERYDAY LIFE

All the fine things in the world are rewards from Nature and our cultural society. Contemporary jewelry art is no exception.

Catherine Truman

Catherine Truman's works boast the theme of her hometown – the twenty kilometre-long coastline of the city of Adelaide, South Australia. It is a landscape of constant change that represents a kind of border territory between human society and the natural world.

She utilizes natural found and industrial objects that she collects from the beach including the remains of marine plants and animals such as shells and sponges, bones, and discarded human debris such as plastic fragments, bottle caps, swimming masks, to create new enigmatic forms that bring into question their origin. At times the viewer is not sure whether the final object is real or manufactured, or whether it comes from the land or the sea. In doing so she invites the viewer to reflect upon the human impact on this natural environment.

1 Eggshells
Brooches, 2013
Oyster shell, otter shells, frilled scallop
shell, thorny oyster shell, glass, paint,
sterling silver, steel
Largest dimension: 125 mm

2 Lush Pink Snail
Object, 2013
Pheasant shell, clay, paint
85×70×45 mm

3 Red Hybrid Shell
Brooch, 2011
Hand-carved English lime wood,
shu niku ink, sterling silver, steel
95×65×30 mm

1 Laboratory Shells and Models
Objects, 2012
Three carvings in English lime,
colored with shu niku ink, clay, shell models
Largest dimension: 100 mm

1 Lush Plants
   Brooches, 2012
   Thermoplastic silicone, sterling silver, steel
   Largest dimension: 160 mm
2 Lush Pink Oyster, Lush Pink Snail, Rococo Escalope
   Objects and brooch, 2013
   Oyster shell, thermoplastic paint, pheasant shell,
   clay, paint, queen scallop shells, sterling silver, steel
   85 x 70 x 45 mm, 85 x 70 x 45 mm, 100 x 100 x 35 mm

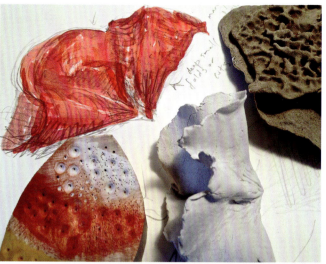

1 | 2
3 | 4

1 The artist working on the final surface
textures of a carving after coloring
2 Sketches and unfinished works
3 Sponge Carvings
Brooches, 2013
Hand-carved English lime wood,
paint, inlaid glass, sterling silver, steel
Largest dimension: 135 mm
4 Corner of artist's studio, Gray Street
Workshop, Adelaide

Despo Sophocleous

Despo Sophocleous challenges us with a question: How would you like to experience a city? Would you take every step following the map in hand, or would you "meander around" aimlessly without a definite destination? Which way is more real? Despo believes that when consciousness vacillates between fantasy and reality, it follows its own path. She favors the perception of subtle interaction between individuals and the city, and relishes the rumination of these oscillating states. Therefore, in her creation, on the one hand, she is so strict to be almost harsh with the structure of the works, such as the exactitude of measurements, values of the drafts and the proportion between constituent elements; on the other hand, however, for the final product, she pursues the vivid interaction and equilibrium among each unit and the lifelikeness exuding naturally from the picture. Just as in the manner of her creative moments, her works are best appreciated allowing vacillation between objectivity and subjectivity, between sense and sensibility, and between the material and the spiritual.

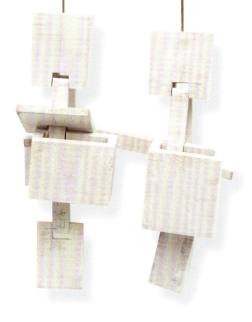

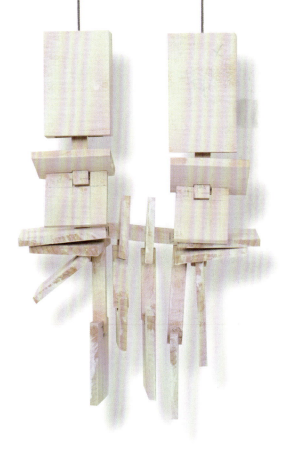

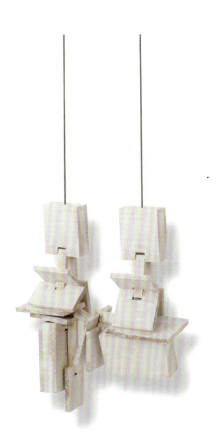

Heejoo Kim

Heejoo Kim intends to share with us various aspects of plants through new materials. They are seen as dualistic or contradictory in her work. The coexistence of familiarity with plant shapes and strangeness from transformed plants stirs the imagination. A mixture of figures reminiscent of animal organs and plant parts comes near to a supernatural mutation. Contrasting complexity, including combinations of familiarity and unfamiliarity, tranquility and fear, passivity and activity, all evolving, is what Kim contains in her jewels.

1 Fifth Season – 1
Brooch, 2011
Enameled copper, hand-dyed leather
80×105×55 mm

2 Fifth Season – 2
Brooch, 2013
Hand-dyed leather
150×110×40 mm

3 Fifth Season – 3
Brooch, 2012
Enameled copper, hand-dyed leather
125×50×35 mm

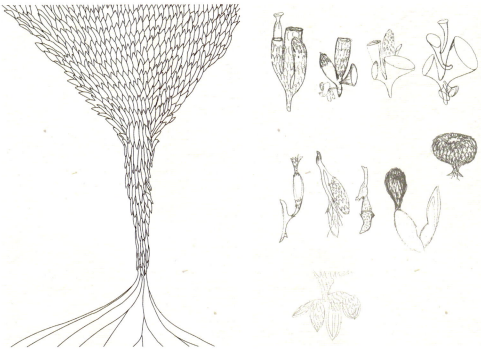

Franz Bette

Franz Bette bases many of his works on field research. In the most primitive and instinctive state, he constructs and processes natural materials in search for inspiration, exploring the unique aesthetics embedded in his constructed models. After that, he returns to the laboratory, conducts experiments and trials again and again, making various models. This process transforms fascinating and exciting emotions into definite materials, structures, and spatial relationships with human body. Lifelike interactions among these elements constitute his unique models of the jewelry.

He believes each creation is closely contingent on the time, place, climate and other environmental elements, which sparks his inspiration; he envisions a preliminary picture for later production with applicable materials. Although he has no studio and improvises all the works like walking a tightrope, he feels the most exciting part of creations rests with field research, during which he rises to challenges in Nature of how to transform inspiration into actual structures.

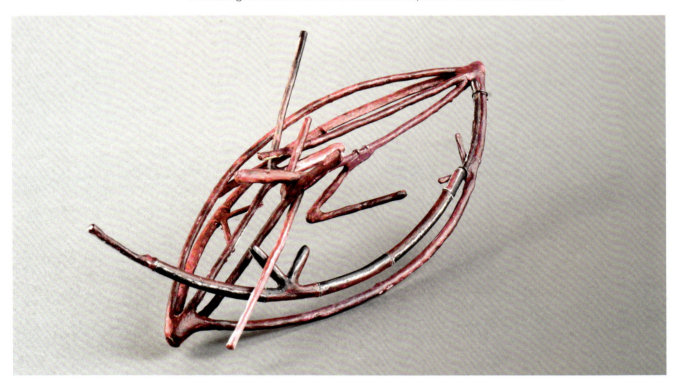

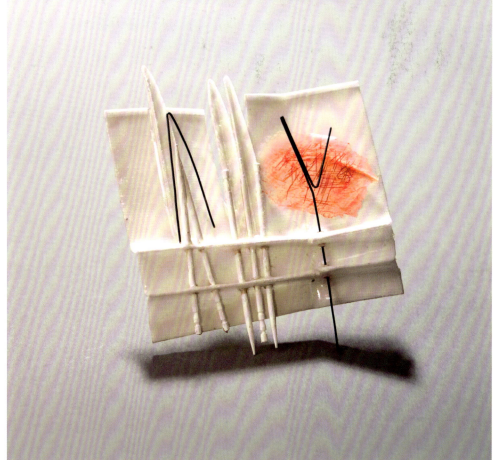

1 Poetic Space – 1
Brooch, 2012
Paper-wrapped mild steel, acrylic paint
200×100 mm

2 Poetic Space – 2
Brooch, 2008
Paper-wrapped mild steel, acrylic paint
230×50 mm

3 Poetic Space – 3
Brooch, 2013
Mild steel, canvas, epoxy, acrylic paint
70×60 mm

4 Poetic Space – 4
Brooch, 2013
Canvas, epoxy, acrylic paint, wood
100×100 mm

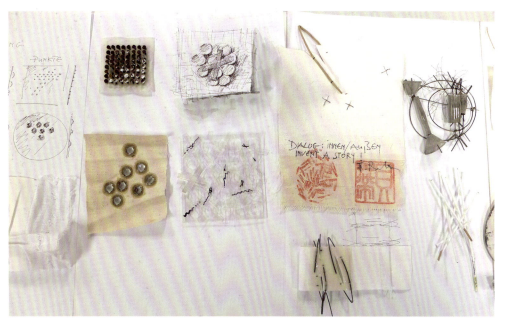

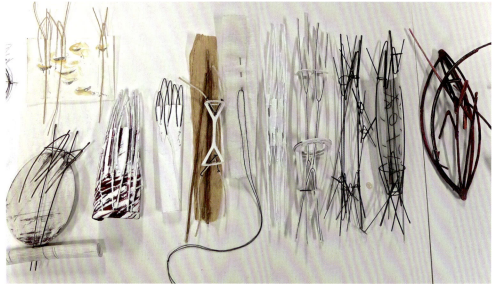

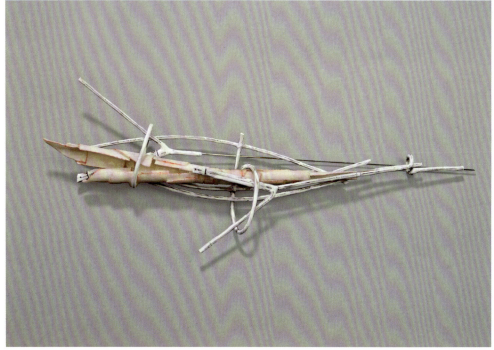

Hanna Hedman

Hanna Hedman is a Swedish jewelry artist in her thirties. Her career is as short as it has been prolific and successful: After concluding her nine-year training in 2008, she hit the ground running with a body of work that was at once singular, technically dazzling, and thematically rich. The work consists of exotic bestiaries, sub-aquatic shrubberies, and anthropomorphic shapes, grown on a strict diet of embossed and cutout sheet metal, and painted in lush dichromatic shades.

1
—
2

1 Balaenoptera Borealis
Brooch, 2011
Silver, oxidized silver, copper, paint
130×100×70 mm

2 Manis Tricuspis
Brooch, 2011
Silver, oxidized silver, copper, paint
160×90×160 mm

Her technical prowess notwithstanding, one suspects that her success was cemented by a strategic use of photography: She has used white-clad models to put her clever assemblages in relief, and offset their talismanic qualities against an ominous air of modern-day normalcy.*

*Text written by Benjamin Lignel, in *HANDSHAKE–12 Contemporary Jewelers Meet Their Hero*

1 | 2 | 3
      4

1 Spheniscus Magellanicus
   Necklace, 2011
   Silver, oxidized silver, copper, paint
   400×185×70 mm

2 Otus Insularis
   Necklace, 2011
   Silver, oxidized silver, copper, paint
   360×170×90 mm

3 Creation process of
   Lipotes Vexillfer

4 Creation process of
   Otus Insularis

1 Black Bile – 3
  Necklace, 2013
  Silver, leather, copper, paint
  610×540×30 mm

2 Black Bile – 4
  Necklace, 2013
  Silver, leather, copper, paint
  560×100×180 mm

3 Black Bile – 5
  Brooch, 2013
  Silver, leather, copper, steel, paint
  350×70×140 mm

4 Creation process of
  "Black Bile" series – 1

1	3
2	4

1 | 2 | 4
3 | 5

1 Black Bile – 6
Necklace, 2013
Silver, leather, copper, paint
430×260×120 mm

2 Black Bile – 7
Necklace, 2013
Silver, copper, paint
330×280×50 mm

3 Creation process of
"Black Bile" series – 2

4 Black Bile – 8
Brooch, 2013
Silver, leather, copper, steel, paint
280×320×110 mm

5 Black Bile
Brooch, 2013
Silver, leather, copper, steel, paint
350×70×90 mm

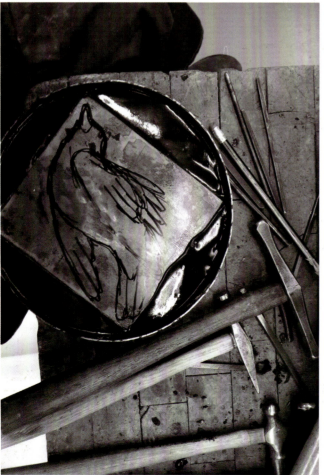
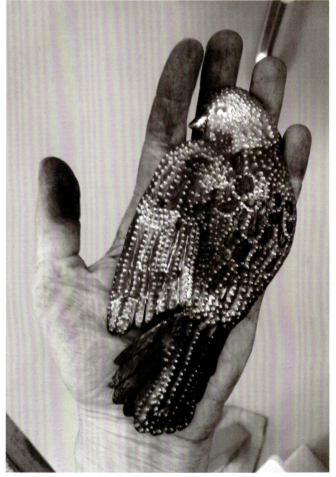

Li Anqi

The expression of "coldness" through the design of jewelry is the essence of Li Anqi's works. Although "coldness" is usually discerned by touch, her creation of these works begins with visual effects and conveys the feeling through visualized shapes. After model production and consequent tests by viewers, Li carefully reviewed large volumes of research, and finally decided on white gypsum as the material for the work. The shape of her work draws from glaciers and minimal geometry so as to avoid interferences with the sense of coldness by irrelevant shapes. Moreover, she compares everybody to an iceberg with only one corner of it revealed to others, since so many parts of human nature are invisible. However, "iceberg" here has no pejorative meaning, but stands neutral in Li's view.

1 | 2
— | 3

1 Cold Mirror – 1
Brooch, 2012
Gypsum, silver
60×80×50 mm

2 Cold Mirror – 2
Brooch, 2012
Gypsum, silver
50×120×50 mm

3 Cold Mirror – 3
Brooch, 2012
Gypsum, silver
50×60×70 mm

Sun Jie

There are two ways to understand "silliness" in literature; these understandings may assist the viewers' appreciation of Sun Jie's works. One is emotionless, resembling what is usually called "slowness;" the other refers to un-shrewdness. Sun's works belong more to the latter. His artwork expresses his personal feelings. He always expects his works to become narrators of fantasies; for visual descriptions of his works, he wishes metaphors like "undiscovered mysterious drafts" or "verses by crazy forest bard" to be applied to each and every piece. He entertains the hope that all his works can at least bring you into his state, if not deliver accurate and beautiful poems to you.

Sun pays close attention to many subtle forms and attributes of materials, yet he doesn't restrict his focus to materials and visual images, but attempts at visual expression of concealed materials. It seems to be a paradox, but what he really desires is to locate the point of equilibrium between new workmanship, new materials, contemporary artistic concepts, and modern aesthetics.

1 | 2
3
4

1-3 Big Fish
Brooch, 2012
Aircraft wood, silver,
steel, gold, car paint
60×50×65 mm

4 "Big Fish" on wearer

1 | 2
3 | 4 **5**

1-2 Mystified
Brooch, 2013
Wood, silver, steel, paint

3 The King
Necklace, 2013
White gold, silver, brass,
crystal diamond HD, wood,
textile, mixed material
120×110×95 mm

4 The King
Brooch, 2013
Silver, brass, steel, wood,
mixed material
90×80×50 mm

5 "The King" on wearer

EYES ON EVERYDAY LIFE ●

1   "The Queen" on wearer
2-4 The Queen
         Brooch, 2013
         Silver, wood, steel, pearl,
         crystal diamond HD, mixed material

Märta Marttson

Jeweler Märta Marttson talks about her work: "Sometimes I see beauty in things that other people find strange or are even repulsed by. I become fascinated when there is something you do not want to see and the feeling you get when you do not want to look at something, yet you still do. My jewelry deals with the tension that lies between attraction and repulsion. I take seemingly inappropriate materials, making ordinary and familiar objects seem extraordinary and unfamiliar."

In the 18th century, many new breeds of animals and plants were discovered, and it was the main era of cabinets of curiosities. People collected rarities because it gave them the feeling of being in the presence of something extraordinary and marvelous. In a world where not many new and exotic breeds are discovered I use dead creatures in my pieces to evoke wonder. The creatures are transformed and reborn and given a new life as objects of astonishment.

1	2	3
		4

1 Fossils – 1
Brooch, 2011
Cicadas, crushed pyrite, resin, silver
150×150×20 mm

2 Fossils – 2
Brooch, 2012
Cicadas, crushed stone, resin, silver
140×150×20 mm

3 Fossils – 3
Necklace, 2012
Cicadas, crushed stone, resin, silver
250×250×20 mm

4 Swarm
Brooch, 2012
Cicadas, crushed stone, glitter, resin, silver
100×90×10 mm

6 Coming out
Brooch, 2011
Beetle, resin, wallpaper,
walnut wood, silver
60×60×30 mm

7 Inside – 1
Brooch, 2011
Copper electroformed beetle,
cubic zirkonias, lacquer, resin, silver
50×40×40 mm

8 Inside – 2
Brooch, 2012
Copper electroformed spider,
cubic zirkonias, lacquer, resin, silver
50×50×30 mm

9 Split
Necklace, 2013
Copper electroformed beetle, driftwood,
cubic zirconias, lacquer, silver
400×200×60 mm

Rachel Darbourne

This body of work by Rachel Darbourne is the result of a collection of deliberately violent actions perpetrated against transitional objects. Initially there is a "murder" manifesting as a deconstruction: this transgression remains difficult to undertake, there is a grieving process for each toy, however it is only when it is complete that the toy becomes open to transformation – into an object that is perhaps sexual, perhaps humorous, perhaps both.

It is the psychological significance of transitional objects (discussed by psychologist D.W. Winnicott in his book *Playing and Reality*) that makes their destruction and reincarnation and the resulting collection of art jewellery all the more emotionally potent.

1 | **4**
2 | **3**   **5** | **6**

1   Lovingly Murdered: Grandad
       Neckpiece, 2013
       Soft toy, rivet, found chain
       80 × 100 × 74 mm

2-4   Source of inspiration

5   Lovingly Murdered: Trophy
       Brooch, 2013
       Soft toy, satin, cord, gold plated
       brass, copper;
       stainless steel, powder coating
       84× 192 × 68 mm

6   Lovingly Murdered: Brown Nose #1
       Brooch, 2013
       Soft toy, polyester filling,
       magnets, flocking
       45 × 48 × 36 mm

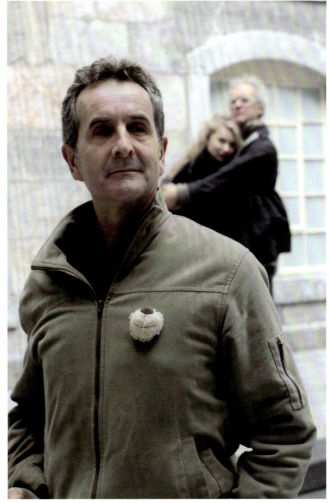

Yin Xiangkun

In memory of his favorite little lizard, Yin Xiangkun initially tried to make animal bone specimens. After meticulous work, he found a complete skeleton so distinctly displayed in front of his eyes which supported the entirety of life, with every bump, curve, and joint so magnificent and incredible, such as created by the prodigious workmanship of Nature. Yin discovered an incomparable beauty of rebirth embedded in the remains of life. After professional art training, he infused these elements into his works; he made lost lives regain their rich emotions and lifelike appearances. These works glow with brilliant appeal instead of remaining dead, dismal "skeletons." Death is just a stage of life, not the end. Yin has no wish to engage in sophisticated arguments or philosophies, but merely hopes that people can appreciate the essence of life and acquire inner peace and tranquility through the works so as to cherish all the truth and beauty in life.

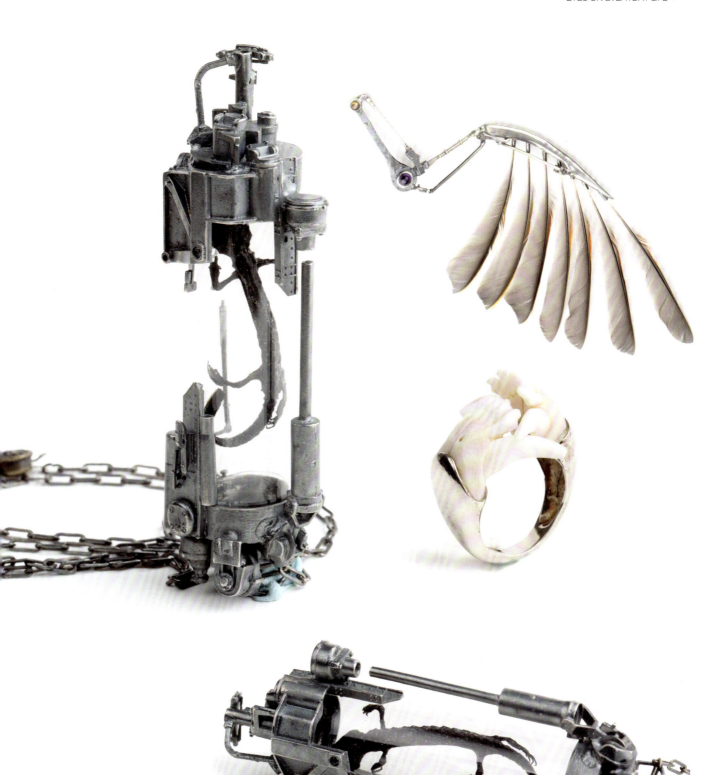

3&6 Untitled
Pendant, 2009
Silver, glass, specimen

4 Leonardo da Vinci's Dream
Brooch, 2009
Silver, feather, amethyst, topaz

5 A Rhapsody of Bones – 2
Ring, 2009
Silver, bone

Yan Rui

Yan Rui received a very precious gift in her childhood – an unabridged *Grimm's Fairy Tales*. It exerted profound influence on Yan's preferences, with Gothic aesthetics and the aesthetics of death in particular, themes that constantly captivate her attention. Similarly, she frequently meditates over the relationship between life and death. In her series, "The Life Cycle of Autumn Cicadas," Yan wishes to convey her understanding of life and death from the perspective of oriental philosophy. "The autumn cicada" represents purity and rebirth in China's ancient culture. It lives as a larva in the dark underground for years, until it breaks out of the earth and flies into the air. This evolution process proves enormously appealing to Yan. She feels that she too seems to live in a human shell while undergoing cycles of joy and sorrow, with death no more being the end of life. Perhaps it is not until the moment when the soul finally leaves the body that the self can be liberated from the cycle of acquisition and of transient easiness and freedom. She desires to break free of the cocoon of the unbearable heaviness of life and soar up into the sky, just like the autumn cicada.

1
—
2

1 The Life Cycle of Autumn Cicadas – 1
   Brooch, 2012
   925 silver, steel needle
   100×90 mm

2 The Life Cycle of Autumn Cicadas – 2
   Brooch, 2012
   925 silver
   120×70 mm

3
—
4
—
5

3 The Fossil
Brooch, 2012
925 silver, steel needle
35×30 mm

4 The Life Cycle of Autumn Cicada – 3
Brooch, 2012
925 silver, steel needle
70×80 mm

5 The Warrior
Ring, 2012
925 silver
50×50 mm

1   The Life Cycle of Autumn Cicada – 4
     Brooch, 2012
     925 silver
     90×90 mm

2-5 Creation process of "The Life Cycle
     of Autumn Cicada" series

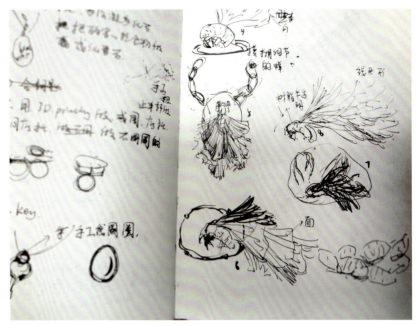

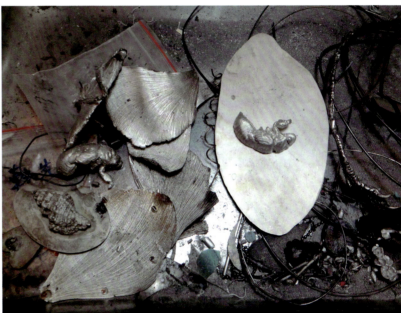

3

MEDITATION ON SELF

Man's civilization is contingent on the higher functions and thoughts of their mental world. Engaging in exploration of a more exalted spiritual world has become the essence of composition for these contemporary jewelry artists.

Agnes Larsson

Agnes Larsson finds inspiration in the powerful opposites that surround us in life, such as life and death, light and dark, surface and depth, and fragility and strength.

She always does practical researches in the material, in this case the carbon. With a carefully selected main material and a theme as a guide, the artist explores the qualities of the material to the utmost with the aim of knowing how much one single material can reveal in reaching the limits of its possibilities.

"Carbo" is a series of necklaces made out of carbon and horsehair. Carbon is a basic material existing in all living things but which we also consider to be dead, burned and charred. Horsehair is a natural material that has connections to a body and a life. The pieces are made out of activated carbon powder and are cast or pressed.

1
—
2

1 Carbo – 1
Necklace, 2011
Carbon, wire, horsehair
430×330×50 mm
2 Carbo – 2
Necklace, 2010
Carbon, horsehair, wire
430×330×50 mm

It is a dark, heavy body of work, but thanks to the specific characteristics of the material it is also light and fragile. In the simple shield-like forms the carbon is no longer recognizable and the fragile horsehair has become reinforcement. The broken pieces with their polished surfaces create a fragile protection against the outside world.

3 | 4
5 | 6

3-4 Carbo – 3
Necklace, 2011
Carbon, horsehair, iron
500×300×150 mm

5 Carbo – 4
Necklace, 2010
Carbon, thread
450×200×50 mm

6 Carbo – 5
Necklace, 2010
Carbon, horsehair
400×150×50 mm

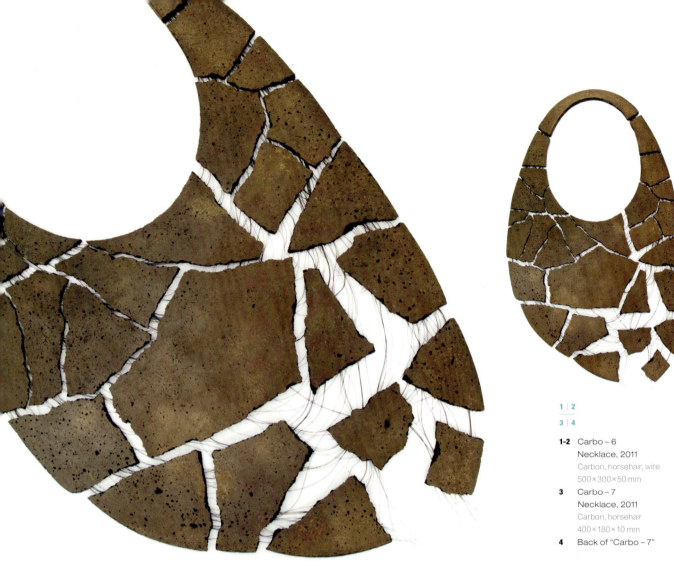

5   Carbo – 9
     Necklace, 2010
     Carbon, horsehair, wire, iron
     500×230×30 mm
6-7 The "Carbo" series on
     wearers

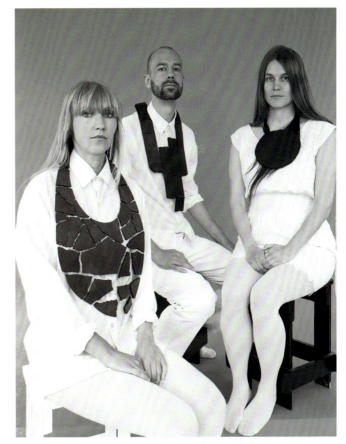

Liu Xiao

Liu Xiao regards the artistic creation of jewelry as both an observation and appreciation of the self. In his mind, requirements of techniques and workmanship during the composition and his own physical and mental states will change in accordance with his inner growth. He records different stages of his creation, observes and appreciates his own states, keeps descriptive track of his behaviors and emotions, comprehends his own subtle variations of self-awareness throughout the whole creation process, and perceives his authentic spiritual changes. He understands these things through the practice of introspection and continuous work day after day, all of which he finally demonstrates in his works.

In his "Rice · Stone" series, Liu attempts to reveal the coarse yet vital spiritual strength of ancient times. Much of his inspiration comes from his research of ritualized visual phenomena in the prehistoric period. This series uses rice and dust as the materials, both of which bear oriental philosophical connotations. In this way he turns transient and insignificant matters into precious and enduring treasures. Through using grains of rice and stones cut by lapidary equipment and properly polished, he infuses substantial spiritual rituals into the entire creation process and repetitive visualized forms. Moreover, the "Rice · Stone" series also extends itself to other artistic media such as photography, behavioral art, writing, and other forms of expression.

1 | 2

1 Rice·Stone – 2120130711
Brooch, 2013
Grains of rice, dust, silver
70×50×40 mm
2 Rice·Stone – The Disappearance
of a Brooch
Brooch, 2013
Grains of rice, dust, silver

3 Rice·Stone – 35130714
Brooch, 2013
Grains of rice, dust, silver
80×50×30 mm

4 Rice·Stone – 33130714
Brooch, 2013
Grains of rice, dust, silver
80×30×40 mm

5 Rice·Stone – 3420131307
Brooch, 2013
Grains of rice, dust, silver
70×40×30 mm

6 Rice·Stone – 40130721
Brooch, 2013
Grains of rice, dust, silver
70×50×40 mm

7-8 "Rice·Stone" series on
wearer

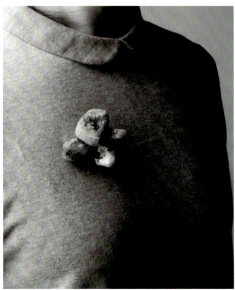

The "Blossoms out of the Withered" and "The Kernel" series mirror Liu's reflection upon the current spiritual status quo of humanity. Nowadays people chase after anything easy, luxurious, and festive in which they indulge themselves, which results in the deterioration of their perception of life and the world at large. It is a common degradation leading to the gradual deprivation of elevating spiritual cultivation for all of humanity. To make matters worse, people's inner spirit is heading towards decline and decadence. Liu wishes to convey through jewelry design a notion that such decadence is dangerously, beyond our control, "radiating a vivid aura."

1 The Kernel – 1
Brooch, 2012
Silver, paper pulp, artificial gems,
natural crystal
70×30×40 mm

2 The Kernel – 2
Brooch, 2012
Silver, paper pulp, artificial gems,
natural crystal
50×30×30 mm

3 Blossoms out of the Withered – 1
    Brooch, 2012
    Silver, paper pulp, artificial gems,
    natural crystal
    50×30×30 mm

4 The Kernel – 3
    Brooch, 2012
    Silver, paper pulp, artificial gems,
    natural crystal
    80×30×40 mm

5 Blossoms out of the Withered – 2
    Brooch, 2011
    Ruby, olivine, crystal, paper pulp, silver
    80×20×40 mm

Ruudt Peters

Ruudt Peters is trained as a jeweler, and chooses to make artwork for the body because, in his words. " I find the interaction between the wearer and the piece to be a much stronger relationship than 'the viewer and the artwork.' When you wear a piece of my work you convey a philosophical message to the world. A piece of jewelry conceived and made with no meaning has no reason to exist."

His work the *Qi* series started with a three-month journey through China to discover Chinese alchemy. During this investigation he discovered Chinese alchemy is the exact opposite of western alchemy. The western is an outer alchemy, with the Chinese being the inner.

"*Qi*" holds the energy of life; Ruudt discovered this by getting in touch with his own during his time in China. He spent those three months making blind drawings. He discovered that his sub-consciousness seems to have direct contact with his belly. Following this investigation, Ruudt took his research back to Amsterdam where he then spent nine months designing and making the collection *Qi*, as well as designing the installation of the work.

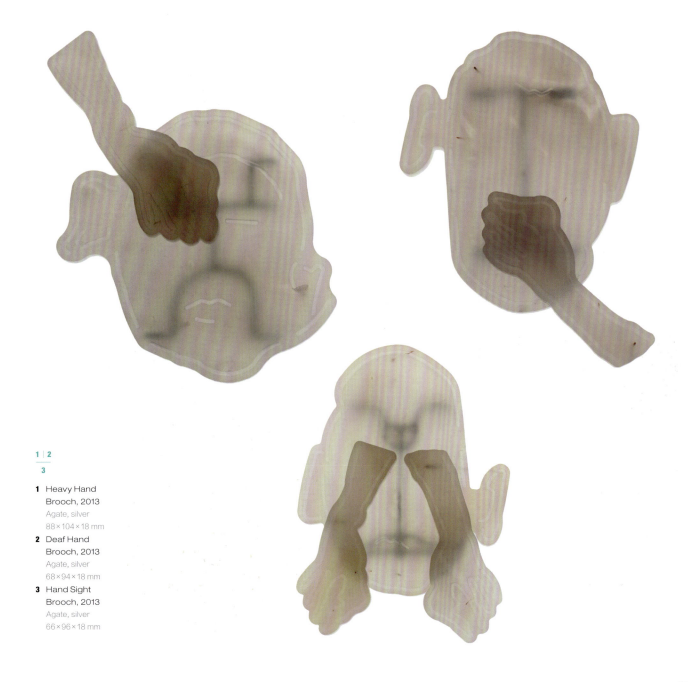

1 | 2
3

1 Heavy Hand
Brooch, 2013
Agate, silver
88 × 104 × 18 mm

2 Deaf Hand
Brooch, 2013
Agate, silver
68 × 94 × 18 mm

3 Hand Sight
Brooch, 2013
Agate, silver
66 × 96 × 18 mm

4

5 | 6

4 Yellow Steam
Brooch, 2013
Bluestone, silver
140×105×12 mm

5 Red Solar
Brooch, 2013
Bluestone, silver
90×96×12 mm

6 White River
Brooch, 2013
Bluestone, silver
80×104×12 mm

1	2	4	5
3		6	7

1 Anima
Necklace, 2011
Aluminium, rubber
100×110×45 mm

2 Corpus
Brooch, 2011
Polyurethane, silver
151×84×40 mm

3 Caput
Brooch, 2011
PU varnish, synthetic resin
70×115×70 mm

4 Gloves
Installation, 2013
Porcelain, paint
410×150×50 mm

5 Brush
Installation, 2013
Porcelain, horsehair
410×150×90 mm

6 Black Power
Installation, 2013
Porcelain, glass
410×150×100 mm

7 Masculinity
Installation, 2013
Porcelain
410×160×50 mm

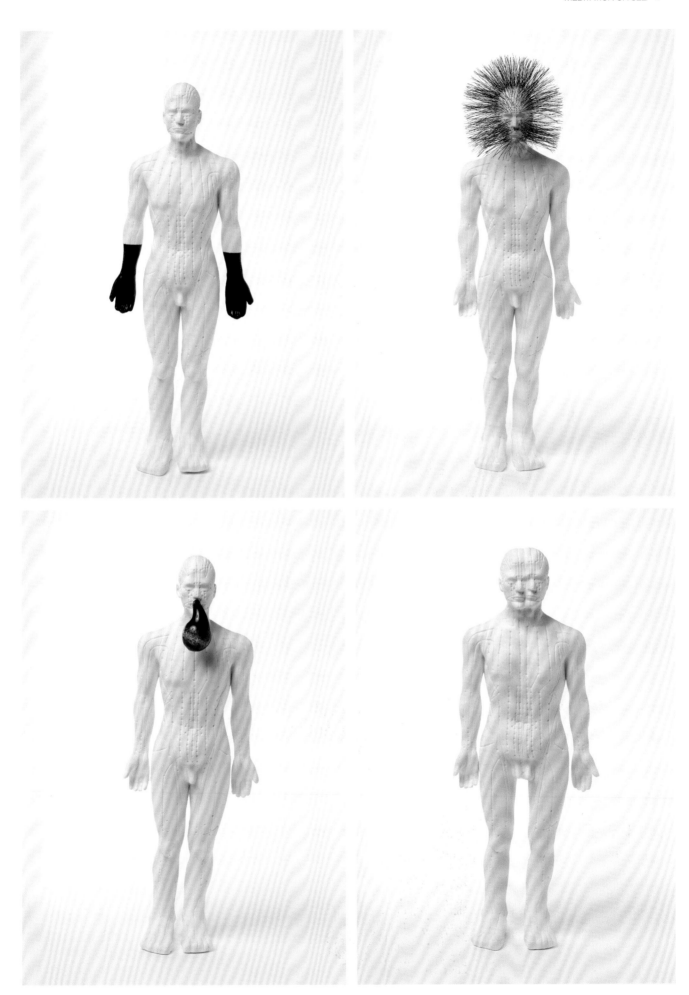

Mari Ishikawa

"Parallel World" represents Mari Ishikawa's contemplation and question of the world outside reality. She draws her inspiration from the subtle perception of the serene atmosphere and flavor in Nature. Where does the "Parallel World" exist? Can one discover the world through time travel? Is it perhaps possible to see this world in a dream? Or does it only exist in one's heart? Mari believes that the world we see is only a part of the entire reality, which is composed of many worlds, existing simultaneously, side by side. We can find "Parallel Worlds" whenever we open our eyes and hearts. They are always with us. During her composition process, Mari chooses various materials and ways to depict the other world in her mind, which is full of thoughts featuring oriental ruminations and outlook on the world.

1	2
3	

1 Hanging Garden – 1
Brooch, 2012
Silver 925, Japanese lacquer (urushi)
85×60×35 mm

2 Hanging Garden – 2
Brooch, 2012
Silver 925 alminium, Japanese lacquer (urushi)
85×60×35 mm
Photography: Dirk Eisel

3 Hanging Garden – 3
Brooch, 2012
Silver 925, Japanese lacquer (urushi)
85×60×35 mm
Photography : Dirk Eisel

Mari notices that old gardens, landscape arts, and old buildings are all fading into oblivion. In that space, the relationships between the interior and the exterior, between the natural and the artificial, turn ambiguous. Time is frozen, but the plants remain. Mari would like to show the silent revolution of plants. Before man built cities, there was only Nature, which we attempt to control according to humanly wishes. Once we stop invading Nature, it would take time to restore it to its original look.

4 **4** Parallel World – 1
5 Necklace, 2012
6 925 silver
500×85×50 mm
Photography: Dirk Eisel

5 Hanging Garden – 4
Necklace, 2011
925 silver, pearls
560×95×40 mm
Photography: Dirk Eisel

6 Parallel World – 2
Necklace, 2012
925 silver, tahiti pearls
500×70×40 mm
Photography: Dirk Eisel

1 Parallel World – 3
Necklace, 2012
925 silver
560×90×40 mm
Photography: Dirk Eisel

2 Parallel World – 4
Brooch, 2011
925 silver
80×100×30 mm
Photography: Dirk Eisel

3 Parallel World – 5
Brooch, 2011
925 silver
90×70×30 mm
Photography: Dirk Eisel

Nanna Grønborg

Nanna Grønborg feels her jewelry is a body-related tool used to comment on problems arising from the collision of the man-made and the conditions of Nature. "This collision," she says, "in combination with the ongoing fusion of cultures, fascinates me; it affects my work, as my own life is a cultural combination."

Nanna approaches her work from two different angles – the practical and the intellectual. She considers her notebook an essential tool, helping to record forms she encounters. Visualizing these and re-assembling them in her mind is the first step. These initial ideas are advanced through drawing, casting moulds, making prototypes, and assembling forms in a continuous, often concurrent flow. Reading and writing accompany the making. All the methods influence and affect each other. It is an elaborate and time-consuming process to bring the work to her level of perfection.

The aesthetic she desires is subtle and minimalist, with marks of the making process. Each piece of her work withholds information that discloses itself through recognition and interpretation.

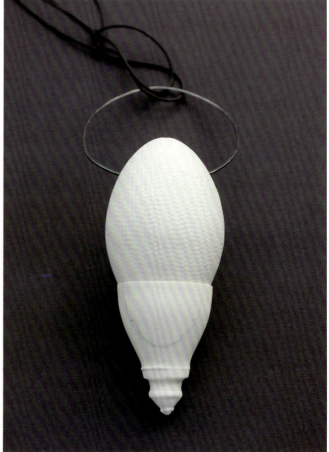

1 | 2   **1** Untitled – 1
         Brooch, 2012
         Porcelain, silver, steel
         110×50×40 mm

         2 Untitled – 2
         Necklace, 2012
         Porcelain, glaze, silver, string
         150×55×40 mm

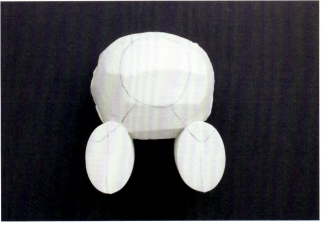

Dorry Hsu

Dorry Hsu's creation of works is just like a fantastic travel, which reveals the essence of life through repetitive deconstruction and recombination. After forty days' dialogue with herself, Hsu gained a deep understanding of fears in life and created the series of "Beauty of Fears" accordingly. Fears are the basic physiological mechanism of human existence, however, if overcoming the reality and triggering fantasy in consequence, they will turn into invisible confining yoke of life.

Her work, "The Multi-foot Worm" demonstrates one of the many fears recorded during the forty days' dialogue with herself. In this series of works, Hsu discusses the relationship between drawing and 3D art and whether it is possible to render 3D drawings as expressive as traditional drawings and statues to convey the creator's emotions and strength with the help of computer softwares.

All of her works begin with "human": the human body and human nature. She endows her works as a whole with expressiveness through ingenious combinations of the human body, costumes and ornaments.

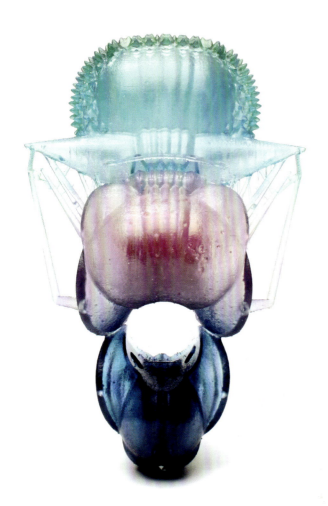

1 | 2

1 The Multi-foot worm – 1
Ring
3D print, resin, colored dye
100×60×40 mm

2 The Multi-foot worm – 2
Ring
3D print, resin, colored dye, silver
70×40×30 mm

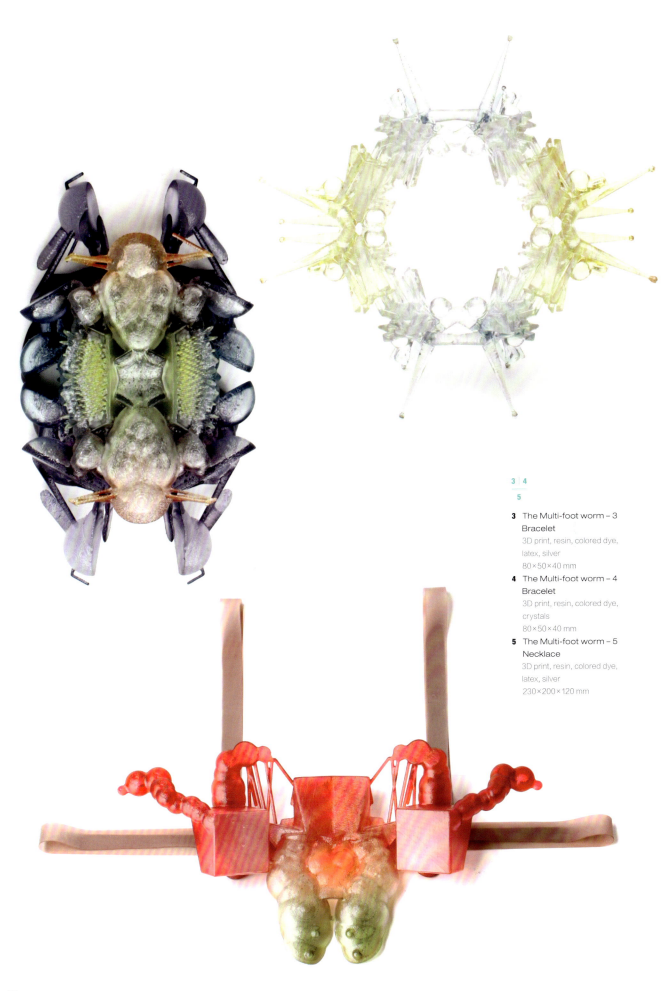

3 | 4
5

3 The Multi-foot worm – 3
Bracelet
3D print, resin, colored dye,
latex, silver
80×50×40 mm

4 The Multi-foot worm – 4
Bracelet
3D print, resin, colored dye,
crystals
80×50×40 mm

5 The Multi-foot worm – 5
Necklace
3D print, resin, colored dye,
latex, silver
230×200×120 mm

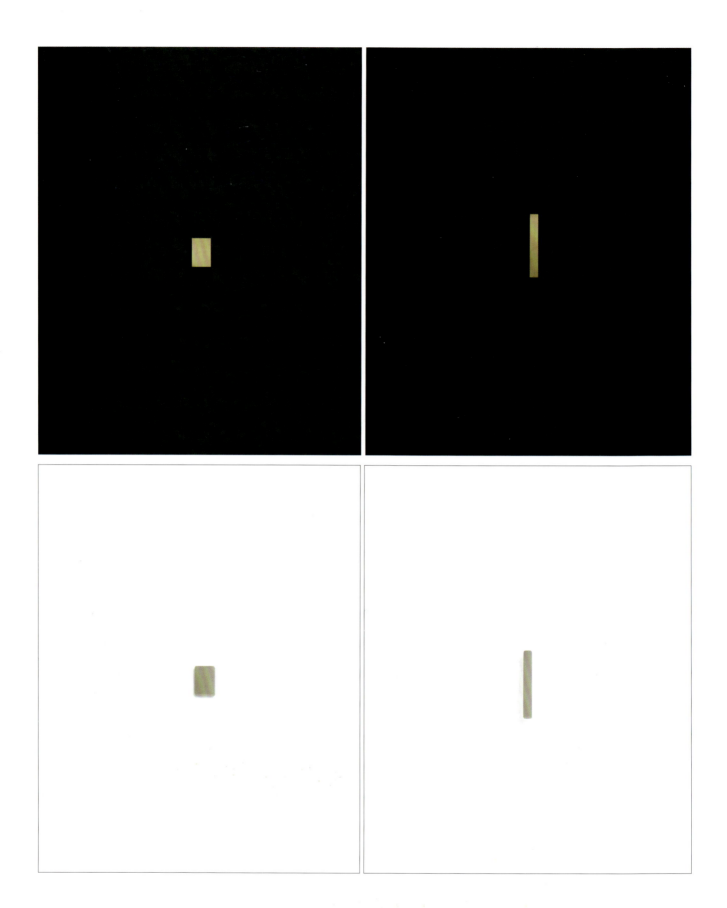

1 Fleeting Moments of Life – 1
Brooch, 2011
Gold
37.5×24×2 mm
11×81×2 mm

2 Fleeting Moments of Life-2
Brooch, 2011
Jade
37.5×24×10 mm
11×81×10 mm

1-4 The "Aesthetic of Fears"
series on wearer

Teng Fei

Every piece of jewelry by Ms. Teng Fei sends forth a story, describing the thoughts and perceptions of the wearer. She believes modern jewelry bears the characteristics of human emotions, and each piece of jewelry must be tailor-made for each individual. Her work doesn't share the traits of traditional design, which attaches great importance to workmanship, materials, and values. Her works are imprinted with deep emotions regarding experiences and understandings of life, legacies of life and the passing of time; she incorporates fleeting moments of life into the forms of her jewelry. By instilling what she experiences about contemporary art into her jewelry design, Teng endows her works with much freedom and an abundance of expressiveness. Moreover, as she once studied material arts in Germany, her works now reflect her unique sensitivity about materials, textures, and details.

1 | 2

1-2 Fleeting Moments of Life
Pendant, 2011
Silver, titanium
100×60 mm

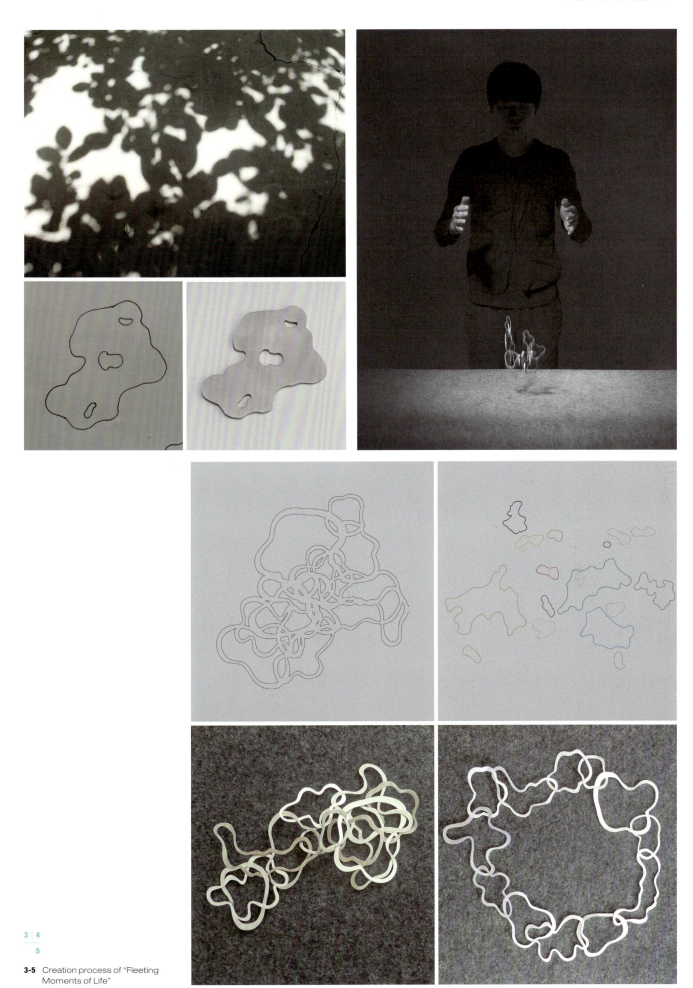

3-5 Creation process of "Fleeting
Moments of Life"

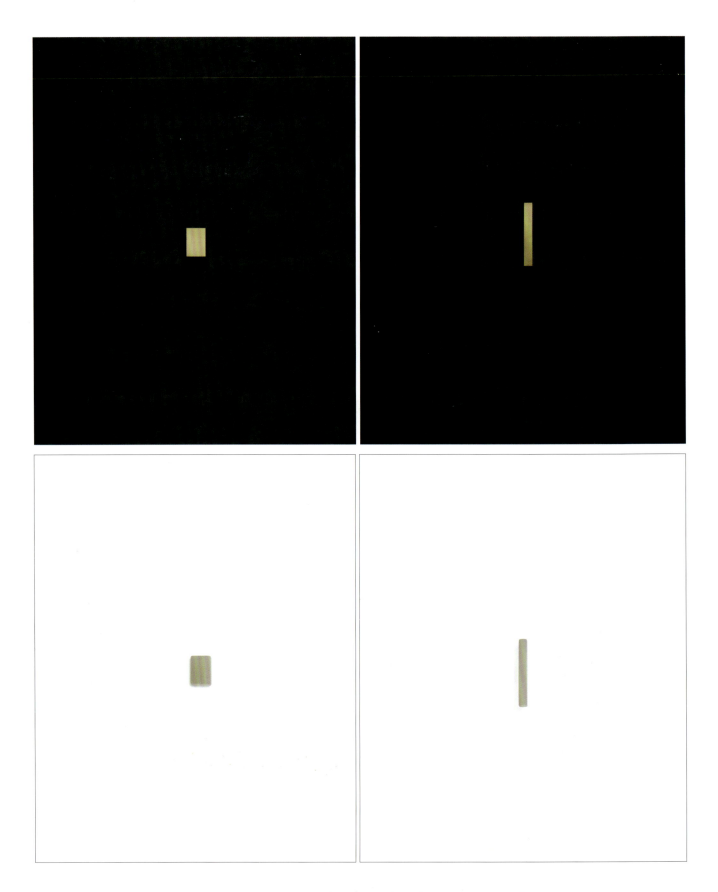

1 Fleeting Moments of Life – 1
Brooch, 2011
Gold
37.5×24×2 mm
11×81×2 mm

2 Fleeting Moments of Life-2
Brooch, 2011
Jade
37.5×24×10 mm
11×81×10 mm

3 Plum Blossoms
Brooch, 2011
Pearls, silver

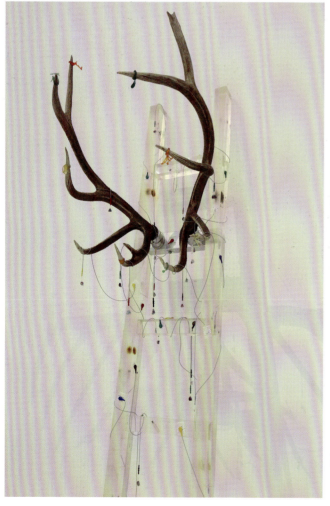

1-3 Solo Exhibition
"Fleeting Moments of Life"

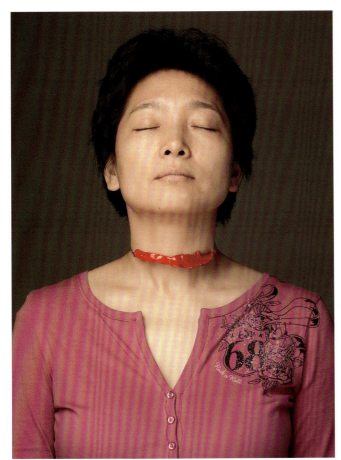

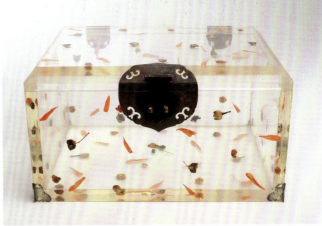

4 That Summer
Sautoir, 2009
Silver, lacquer
Diameter: 100 mm

5 Chinese Box
Installation, 1996
Organic glass, dried flowers
500×350×280 mm

6 Warm Dream
Installation, 1994
Silk, light
50 m^2

7 Spring
Installation, 1993
Horsehair, clear water
Diameter: approx. 900 mm and 180 mm

Shen Yi

Shen Yi finds that in this age of material affluence, her inspiration derives from meditations on "objects" around us. Such contemplation is not just an inspection of these objects, but also a penetrating disclosure of humane states, relationships, emotions, and stories through these inanimate objects, which bear numerous, and tangled connections with the lives involved.

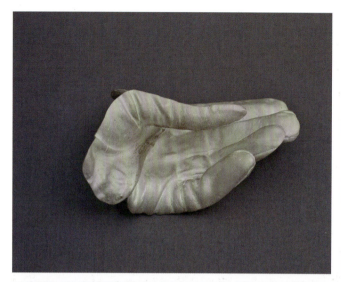

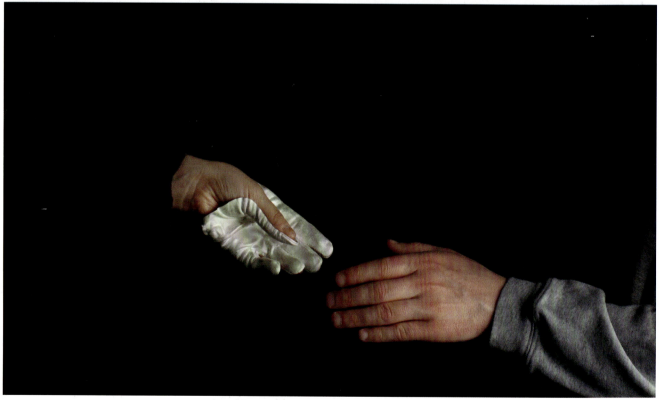

1	2
3	4

1&3 Ourselves Beside Me – 1
Object
Silver, flocking
100×170×40 mm
A faux glove offers opposite tactile senses between the wearer and the toucher

2&4 Ourselves Beside Me – 2
Brooch 1, 2
Silver, leather, steel wire
50×50×30 mm
Mirror-like surfaces that only reflect distorted faces

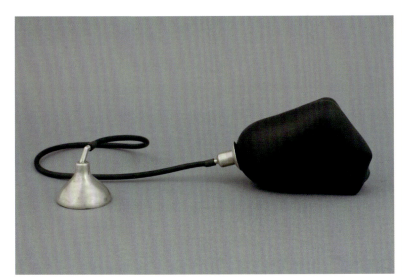

1-2 Ourselves Beside Me – 3
Kiss Machine
Silver, rubber, silicone
300×50×40 mm
An object offers a five-second-kiss
experience when wearers squeeze the
air out of the rubber pump and press the
silver sucker tight to their skin

3 Ourselves Beside Me – 4
Bracelet
Silver, leather, jasmonite
270×200×170 mm
A heavy bag, unable to be opened,
it is useless – just like the handbags
that girls bring to parties

4 Ourselves Beside Me – 5
Necklace
Silver, leather, jasmonite
500×200×170 mm
A bag used in daily life usually is the
best showcase to display and carry the
owner's personality

Wu Junjin

Traditional Chinese painting attaches great importance to the consummate command of "strength." While drawing with vigor and firmness, a flexibility and tenderness is also called for. During traditional Chinese painting, the drawer wields his ink brush as quickly as the wind so that, in a blink after dipping the brush, a magnificent picture appears on the paper, with exquisite effects of light and shade veiled in a pristine and dignified atmosphere. Wu Junjin refers to this style in her jewelry design with a view to discovering mutual benefits and references between them. She sticks with one single color, one single material, and even a sole technique (i.e., carving), which proves to be both constraints and opportunities at the same time. How to generate infinity out of finitude becomes the proposition. During the creation, she needs to maintain the strength throughout the process until all energy is exhausted, In conclusion, whether it is traditional Chinese painting or jewelry design, the artworks share the pursuit of expressiveness and flexibility.

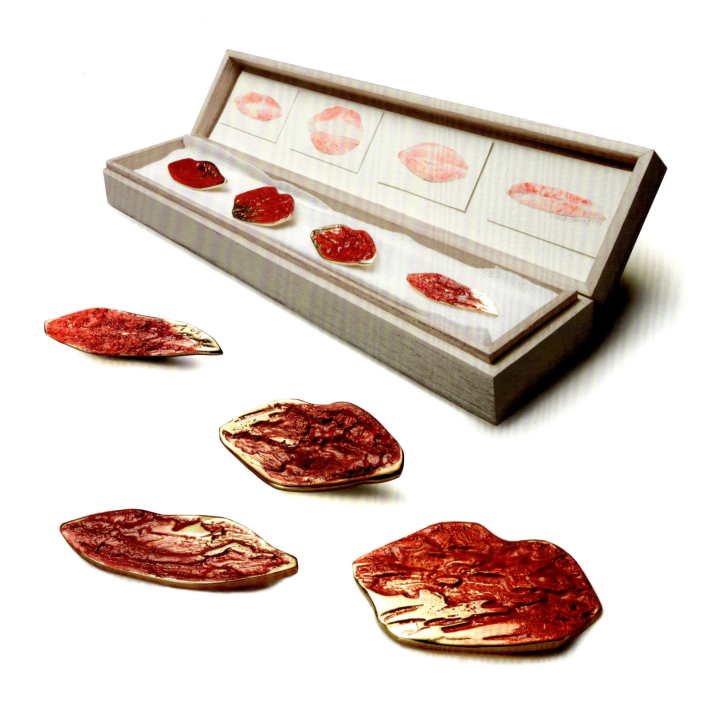

1 │
2 │ 3
4 │ 5

1 "Release of Silence," from
"Quiet Out Loud" series
Brooch, 2012
Silver, gold, resin, handmade wood
box, lipstick, cashmere felt
258×60×16 mm

2 "Release of Silence," from
"Quiet Out Loud" series – 1
Brooch, 2012
Silver, gold, solid lip gloss, resin
40×11×2 mm

3 "Release of Silence," from
"Quiet Out Loud" series – 2
Brooch, 2012
Silver, gold, solid lip gloss, resin
37×20×2 mm

4 "Release of Silence," from
"Quiet Out Loud" series – 3
Brooch, 2012
Silver, gold, solid lip gloss, resin
45×18×2 mm

5 "Release of Silence," from
"Quiet Out Loud" series – 4
Brooch, 2012
Silver, gold, solid lip gloss, resin
40×25×2 mm

6 │
7 │ 8

6 "Continuity and Inspiration," from
"Quiet Out Loud" series – 1
Brooch, 2012
Wood, pigments, lacquer,
stainless steel
105×78 mm

7 "Continuity and Inspiration," from
"Quiet Out Loud" series – 2
Brooch, 2012
Wood, pigments, lacquer,
stainless steel
114×45 mm

8 "Continuity and Inspiration," from
"Quiet Out Loud" series – 3
Brooch, 2012
Wood, pigments, lacquer,
stainless steel
185×38 mm

1 Moment of Force – 1
Brooch, 2011
Oxidized silver, copper
81×53×11 mm

2 Moment of Force – 2
Brooch, 2011
Oxidized silver, copper
80×50×11 mm

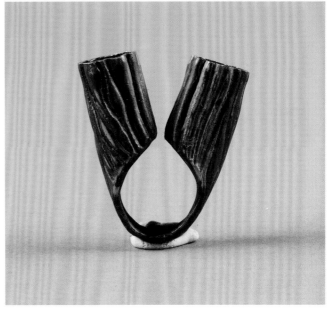

3 | 4

5

3 Moment of Force – 3
Brooch, 2011
Oxidized silver, copper
39×33×20 mm

4 Moment of Force – 4
Brooch, 2011
Oxidized silver, copper
40×37×11 mm

5 Moment of Force
– Source of inspiration
2009 – 2013
500×300 mm

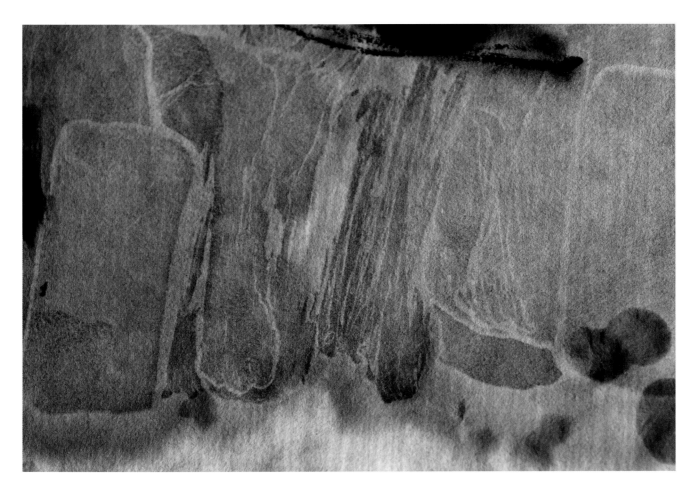

Wen-Hsien Hsu

Numbers and dimensions can be used to explain many things in life, and serve as the reference systems for people to make specific decisions. However, once emotions are involved, it is impossible for people to make decisions in line with logic instead of doing something irrational, which is usually the case.

Consequently, Wen-Hsien Hsu wishes that emotions could be quantified as well. Via knotting various details of life into the fabrics, combined with other measures of quantifying feelings, she has managed to depict people's emotional relationships with existing methods. Such treatments allow viewers or wearers to engender various feelings or opinions in accordance with their own preferences, which may help them to acquire some new understandings of life. Wen-Hsien wishes to instill such original concepts into current objects so as to expose the abstract beauty of these objects beyond their concrete forms.

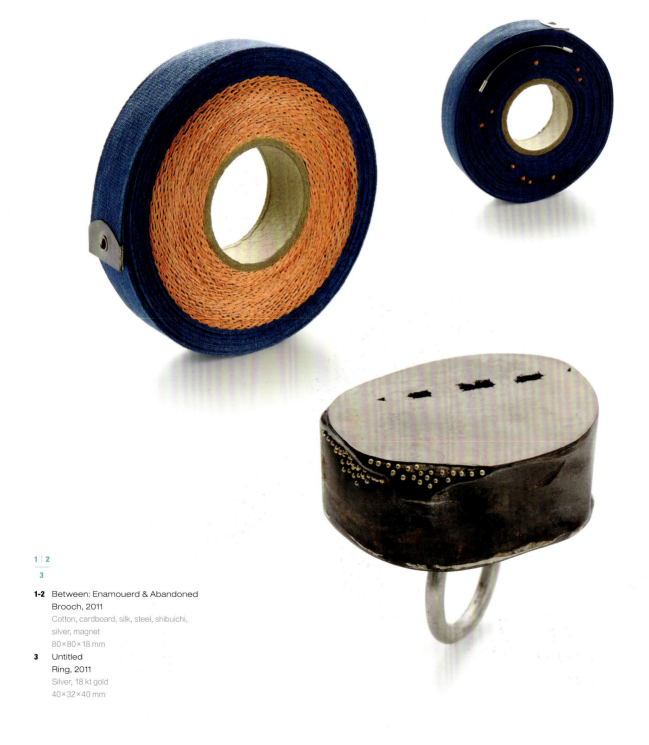

1 | 2
3

1-2 Between: Enamouerd & Abandoned
Brooch, 2011
Cotton, cardboard, silk, steel, shibuichi,
silver, magnet
80×80×18 mm
3 Untitled
Ring, 2011
Silver, 18 kt gold
40×32×40 mm

4 | 5
6

4 Between: Passion & Apathy
Brooch, 2011
Cotton, cardboard, silk, steel,
shibuichi, silver
83×83×36 mm

5 Between: Sense & Sensibility
Brooch, 2011
Cotton, silk, steel, shibuichi,
silver, magnet
100×95×18 mm

6 Between: United & Divided
Necklace, 2011
Cotton, silver
68×60×17 mm

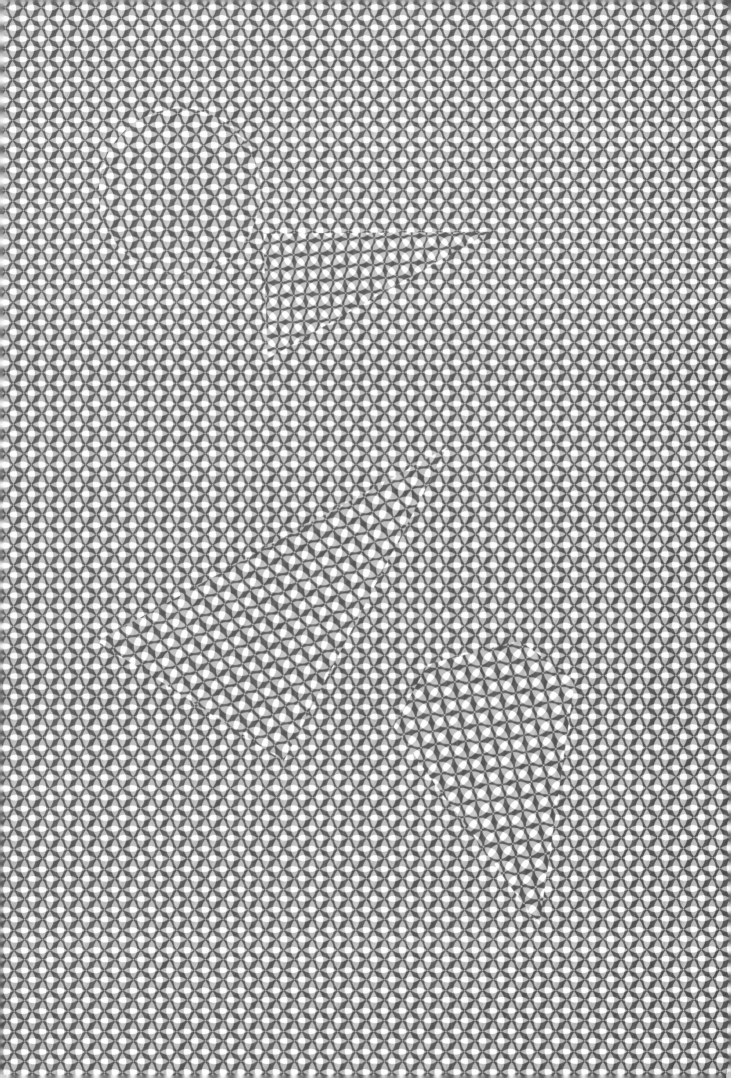

4

QUESTION BASED
ON EXPLORATION

During the collision of arts with new technologies and novel concepts, artists have continued to create, exploring on a wider scope.

Benjamin Lignel

Contemporary jewelry is a relatively new phenomenon - it emerged in Europe and the US during the 1960s - defined to some extent by this paradox: a young field with an extremely old tradition. Over the following decades, the practice has progressively branched out from its iconoclastic roots, and formulated the lines of investigation that continue to define it today: the field's mixed origins (craft, art, design) and the ambivalent status of what it produces: a class of objects that are non-functional yet body-related, poised between the social and the intimate. It is against such a background that Benjamin Lignel's artistic creation, caring less for whether it falls into the category of art or that of jewelry, came into being.

"Priapus" (2013) is a work of installation art, which composes a slightly bending mannequin facing a tiny human figure whose penis is perpetually erect. A metal chain links the tiny figure with the larger mannequin. Through the deadlock between the two, Benjamin wishes to express his own unfortunate charisma and display masculine power in public. He holds that it is because of this pathetic yet exciting power that males are eligible to be called men.

1 Priapus
  Made-up Mannequin, 2013
  Installation
  Found clothes, gold- plated tin necklace
  Photography: Florian Kleinefenn
  Courtesy of NextLevel Galerie

2 Suppléments
  Brooch, 2012
  Gold-plated tin, stainless steel
  Photography: Lionel Gustave
  Courtesy of NextLevel Galerie

3 Priapus (detail)

His series "The Complements" represents an additional object attached incongruously to the body, playing the same role as adornments used for praying. Therefore, the pieces of this series are not replicas of other ornaments, but represent desirable characteristics people wish to possess. Although they may appear coarse and seemingly unwanted or even redundant, the style of "nonconformity with the era" they represent is the very reason why Benjamin created them. Just as other "extensions to the body" displayed in the pictures, their emphasis rests not with charming appearances, but with clumsy, wishful and exaggerated forms, which provide eccentric highlights for human social exchanges.

"Yoni" is complementary to "Lingam." "Lingam" is a re-creation on the theme of worshipping a phallus as a symbol of the god Shiva, one of three Hindu deities. The work submitted by Benjamin is a foldable penis (subtitled "Intelligent Toys in the 21st century"), and the same method was passed down to "Yoni." Meanwhile, he decided to employ the original forms of "Yoni" – a Kaaba circular stone with an extending beak which carries a phallus in the middle as the base to design splendid exhibition halls.

1 | **2**
   | **3**

1 Yoni – Third Edition
  2013
  Installation
  Pearls, gold–plated steel, gold
  Photography: Florian Kleinefenn
  Courtesy of NextLevel Galerie

2 Lingam and Yoni
  2009, 2013
  Lingam: gold–plated silver,
  stainless steel, nylon
  Yoni: pearls, gold–plated
  steel, gold
  Photography: Lionel Gustave,
  Courtesy of NextLevel Galerie

3 Reflective Objects
  Brooch, 2013
  Gold- plated tin, stainless steel
  Photography: Enrico Bartolucci
  Courtesy of NextLevel Galerie

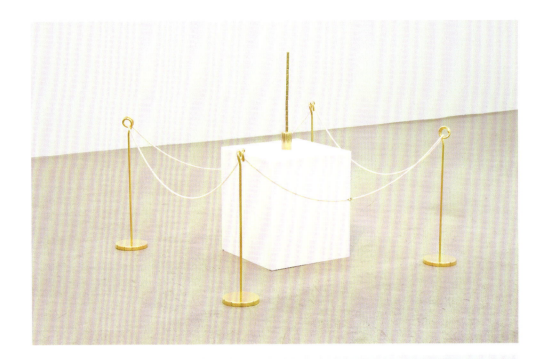

The series of "Reflective Objects" are cylindrical gilded brooches with a full spectrum of heights and sizes, which resemble parts and components of industrial products with a wide range of sizes. In this series Benjamin showcases his works in the way of traditional shoe stores: piling shoe boxes with shining trademarks on the shelves to form a special layout, then following this layout to arrange this series of brooches side by side according to their sizes. He expects to transfer these conspicuous and shinning objects and arrange them in a natural order similar to the order in numbering, so as to present the most ordinary and unobtrusive display.

He Jing

He Jing's works always generate a sense of "to be continued," which is the very state of her pursuit of knowledge. She always maintains a clear and skeptical mind towards jewelry concepts that others take for granted, and infuses such practices of pondering and candid questioning into her jewelry design.

The series, "Brooch," is an experiment of fashioning brooches by combining ready–made objects. She wishes to understand the possibilities between "being useful and being useless," the correlations between "function and aesthetics," and personal experiences of them. This series is the crystallization of He's constant exploration of the relationship between forms and functions of industrial products, such as how functions, besides aesthetic requirements, determine the form. She aspires to understand why these forms matter and how people use them, evenif it is in an incorrect manner.

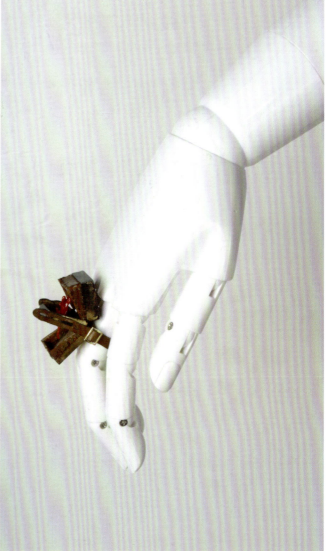

1 | 2   3 | 4
           5

1 Portrait of Temperament – 1
Ring, 2007
Silver, glass

2 Portrait of Temperament – 2
Ring, 2007
Silver, copper, glass, leather

3 Portrait of Temperament – 3
Ring, 2007
Silver, leather

4 Portrait of Temperament – 4
Ring, 2007
Silver, copper, leather

5 Portrait of Temperament – 5
Ring, 2007
Silver, glass, leather

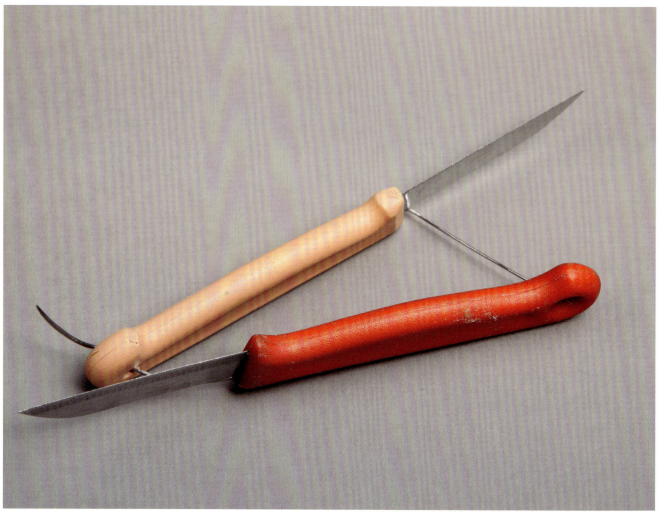

```
    1      5
 ——————  ———————
 2 | 3 | 4  6 | 7 | 8
            9
```

1 Brooch – 1
Brooch, 2013
Ready- made (knife), alloy wire,
stainless steel wire
110×60×10 mm

2 Brooch – 2
Brooch, 2013
Ready- made (whisk, opener),alloy
wire, stainless steel wire
110×60×10 mm

3 Brooch – 3
Brooch, 2013
Ready- made (opener), ally wire,
stainless steel wire
130m×40×40 mm

4 Brooch – 4
Brooch, 2013
Ready- Made (opener), alloy wire,
stainless steel wire
120×70×10 mm

5 Brooch – 5
Brooch, 2013
Ready- made (apple corer), stainless wire
90×20×20 mm

6 Brooch – 6
Brooch, 2013
Ready- made (wine opener), remanium
140×40×20 mm

7 Brooch – 7
Brooch, 2013
Ready- made (plastic spoon), tablecloth
clip), Remanium
120×60×40 mm

8 Brooch – 8
Brooch, 2013
Ready- made (Jalema clip), remanium
30×80×10 mm

9 "Brooch" Series on display
Photography: DAN/NAD

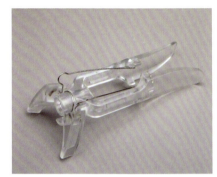

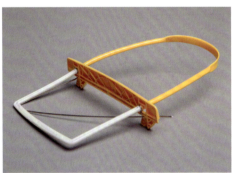

Iris Eichenberg

Wearing and using jewelry allows it to relate with the body, which engenders psychological suggestions and associations. These associations may be visual or tactile, or even olfactory. Mixing and combining various perceptions constitute the visual language of Iris Eichenberg's works. Her works, ascending beyond traditional attributes and forms of jewelry, discuss the relationship between jewels and the body and between jewelry and its surroundings in terms of materials. Her works are related to the body, yet not just the physical body, but also the body in historical, social, and political contexts.

She believes that people base their judgments of different environments on their subconscious awareness of senses of touch, sounds, sizes, odors, and temperatures. Yet, how do people understand and perceive things around them? Their perception is based on feelings, the conscious, and subconscious interweaving together; it is from this that Iris derives her inspirations of creation. The interrelations among these three elements also become a main theme for Iris' creation.

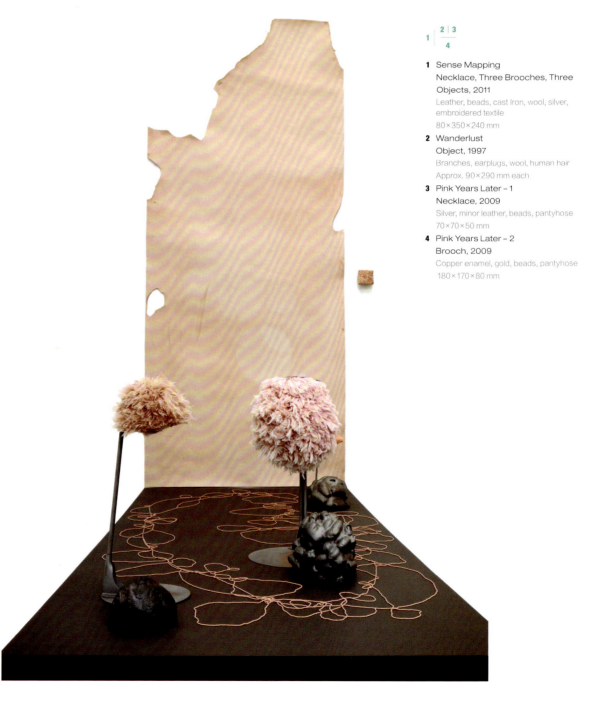

1	2	3
		4

1 Sense Mapping
Necklace, Three Brooches, Three Objects, 2011
Leather, beads, cast Iron, wool, silver, embroidered textile
80 × 350 × 240 mm

2 Wanderlust
Object, 1997
Branches, earplugs, wool, human hair
Approx. 90 × 290 mm each

3 Pink Years Later – 1
Necklace, 2009
Silver, minor leather, beads, pantyhose
70 × 70 × 50 mm

4 Pink Years Later – 2
Brooch, 2009
Copper enamel, gold, beads, pantyhose
180 × 170 × 80 mm

Iris wishes to learn from her own works; she looks to discover surprises and feel amazed. She goes so far as to force herself to create with unfavorable materials; she meticulously observes the power of attraction and repulsion triggered on this occasion, and the most subtle states in the transformations of the materials. All jewels, utensils, and installation artworks designed by Iris are combined deliberately through limited materials and colors. She believes works with one sole color are the most appropriate creation. Through classification of incompatible modeling elements, she reconstructs their expressiveness. It is a challenge to apply a single color within limited space, as the goal is not for settlement of the conflicts among various materials, but for a better coexistence of the material and the form.

Hilde De Decker

Hilde De Decker's work is not only an object-based practice but also a spatial one: The body serves not as the exclusive destination for jewelry, but as the reference to operate in a human-scale environment. It comes as no surprise that she studied interior architecture for two years before starting her training as a jewelry artist at the College of Art & Design, St. Lucas University Antwerp. The metaphor of the home says a lot about her work, which is an investigation of creating value when diving into the dense materiality of everyday life. Indeed, Hilde's work has to be approached as a sensorial architecture made up of several chambers. Like successive still lives, they reveal an internal logic underlying the artist's recurrent themes: Jewelry as a perspective to reflect on value, domesticity and conceptualism, and the beauty of the obsolete.

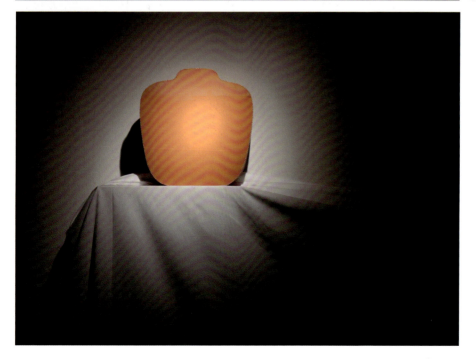

1	2	4
3	5	

1-2 "Jommeke," from "On the Move" series
Object, 2010
Cartoon, ink, metal support
Photography: Rikard Westman

3 "Display," from "On the Move" series
Object, 2010
Cardboard, canvas, cotton
Photography: Rikard Westman

4 Overview of exhibition "On the Move" in Gallery Platina, Stockholm, 2010
Photography: Rikard Westman

5 Overview of exhibition "On the Move" in Gallery Marzee, Nijmeghen, 2010
Photography: Hanneke van Hage

Wedding ring turns up in potato after twenty years – this was the starting point for Hilde's project, "For the Farmer and the Market Gardener." Reality defies the imagination. The reverse may be true too. But that demands three or four months of intensive work: building and whitewashing a greenhouse, selecting and cultivating plants; digging, weeding, raking, ventilating the greenhouse and – not to be forgotten – watering and feeding. And then the jewels: First experiment with the artist's own souvenirs and others' trinkets, then wait for the results before testing with gold and silver. How does a vegetable react to precious metal? To being pierced, to a gold leaf, or silver thread? Ultimately design jewelry that grows into the vegetables. Or is it the other way around? Fit the jewelry over the tender young fruit, not too early, not too late. Adjust, intervene, and lead every week, or even every day. Create new jewelry every week, and follow the rhythm of the vegetables. Finally, harvest silver and gold some weeks later.*

1	
2 | 3	

1 For the Farmer and the Market Gardener – 1
Ring, from 1999 on
Silver ring, eggplant
Photography: Hilde De Decker

2 For the Farmer and the Market Gardener – 2
Ring, from 1999 on
Silver, tomato
Photography: Hilde De Decker

3 For the Farmer and the Market Gardener – 3
Ring, from 1999 on
Found gold ring with diamonds, tomato
Photography: Hilde De Decker

* Text written by Monica Gaspar

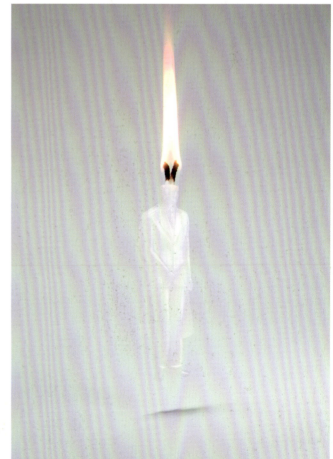

4 | 5 **4-6** Candle Collier
6   Necklace, 2007
       Wax, cotton, box
       Photography: Eddo Hartmann

Kim Buck

With his "Precious Stones" project, Kim Buck focuses on and challenges the concept of value and the traditional understanding of value in his profession. The normal market mechanism sees rarity and purity as the main parameters concerning the value of materials. It's about supply and demand. Low supply equals high price. The real value of a piece of jewelry is mostly what he terms "relational value." It is the value that relates to a personal history, symbolism, affection, faith, and superstition. The piece of jewelry is given an almost talismanic character.

In this project, Kim used stones found in Nature in many places in Denmark. They are shaped and polished by Nature. We all know the fascination we feel by looking at the stones on the beach, picking some up, and saving them – they have a value to us, which is strangely indefinable, yet genuine. Kim has not done any other work to these stones other than to drill holes for attaching mountings that make the stones into pendants. But each stone is carefully described in a certificate in which the place it was found, type of stone, weight, and other relevant information are registered with a photo and coordinates, as a reference to the certificates that many serious companies and institutions issue.

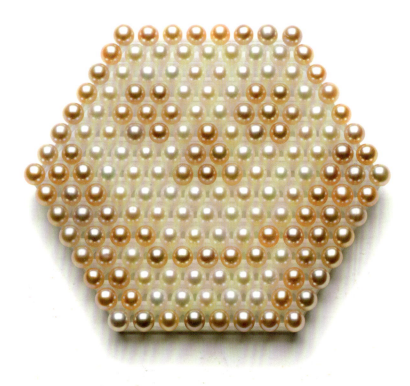

1 | 2
3

1 Pearl Plate
Brooch, 2007
Cultured pearls, polyamide, 18 kt gold
Photography: Anders Sune Berg

2 Heart of Steel
Pendant, 2010
Photography: Kim Buck

3 Copy
Ring, 2007
750 gold
Photography: Anders Sune Berg

4 Pumpous – 1
2012
999,9 gold filled with hot air
Photography: Kim Buck

5 Pumpous – 2
2012
999,9 gold filled with hot air
Photography: Kim Buck

6 Pumpous (Colored)
2012
999,9 silver, powder coating
Photography: Kim Buck

Wu Mian

Wu Mian works under the context of traditional jewelry mass production, discussing the rules that people feel accustomed to, the judgment of standard and defected goods, as well as the accurate control given to us by industrialization.

First, wax injection machines and silicon molds are used to mass-produce standard wax copies, which will then be cast into metal jewelry. During the process there will be defective wax copies. These imperfect ones will be melted into liquid and injected again so they become standard products.

A special relationship between this work and traditional jewelry is expected to be established via the mass production of wax injection, providing a new perspective on our views of defects, accidents, and other uncontrollable factors.

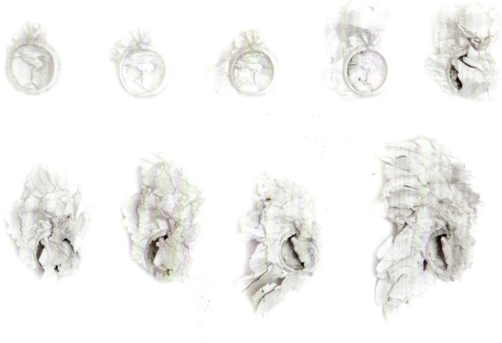

1
—
2   3

1   Creation process of
         "Starting from a Ring"
2-3   Starting from a Ring – 1
         2012
         Silver
         40×90×30 mm

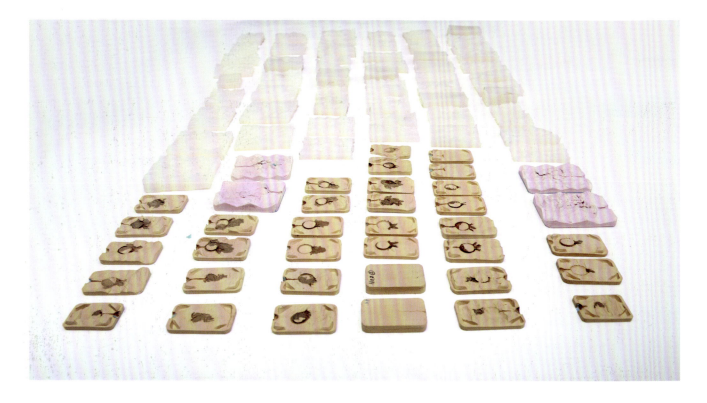

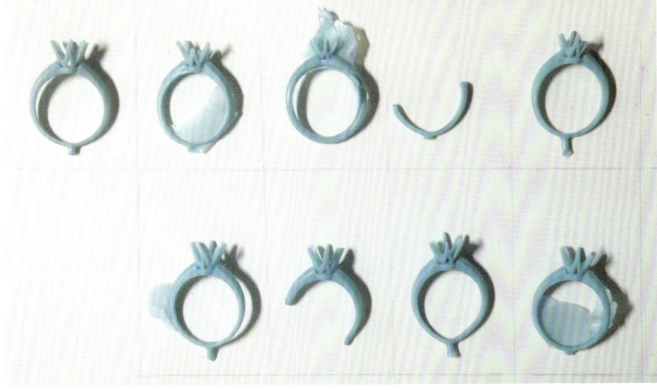

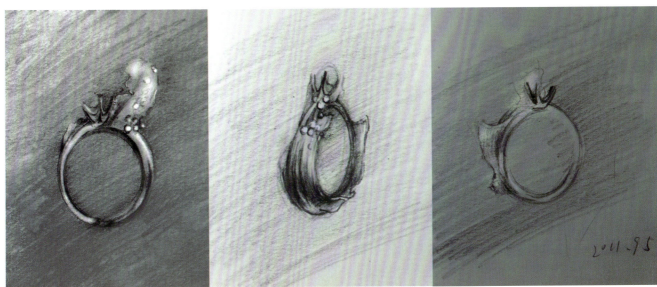

Tiffany Parbs

Tiffany Parbs' practice explores the surface and movement of the body, highlighting the inherent capabilities, limitations, and natural features. "I am intrigued by the transitional relationship between body and object, natural aging processes and the way the body assimilates external influences and embellishments over time. The main intent of my work aims to invite examination of articles allowed into intimate space, and to encourage the viewer to reassess and reconsider contextual aspects of objects when placed in relation to the body," she explains.

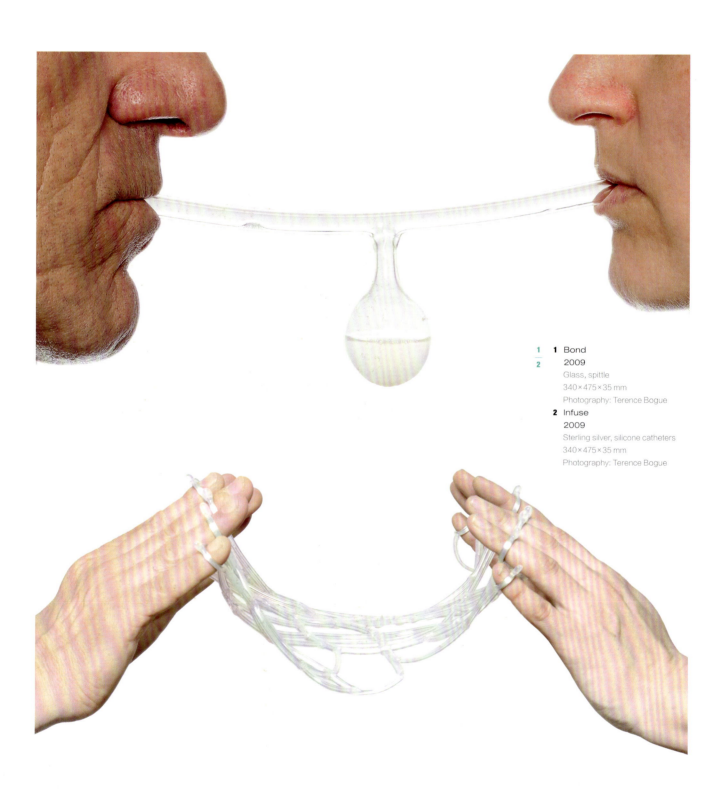

1
2

1 Bond
2009
Glass, spittle
340×475×35 mm
Photography: Terence Bogue

2 Infuse
2009
Sterling silver, silicone catheters
340×475×35 mm
Photography: Terence Bogue

3   Precious
         2009-2013
         24 kt gold, lipstick compound, digital print
         930 × 1,290 mm
         Photography: Terence Bogue

4-5 Flow
         2013
         22 kt gold leaf, plastic, digital print
         210 × 295 mm

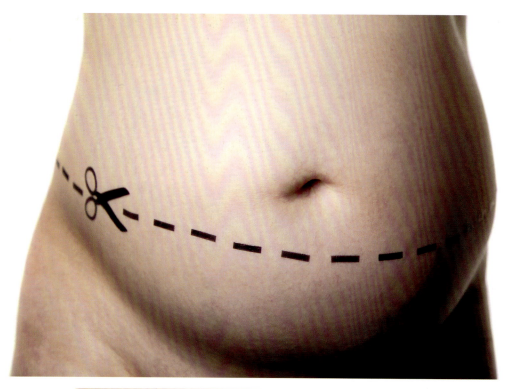

INGREDIENTS: MELATONIN, SEROTONIN, THYROXINE, TRIIODO...
NOREPINEPHRINE, DOPAMINE, ANTIMULLERIAN HORMONE, AD...
HORMONE, ANGIOTENSINOGEN, ANGIOTENSIN, HEPCIDIN, LEPTIN, ...
ATRIAL-NATRIURETIC PEPTIDE, CALCITONIN, ANITDIURETIC HORMONE
RELEASING HORMONE, ERYTHROPOIETIN, FOLLICLE-STIMULATING HOR...
FACTOR 19, GASTRIN, GHRELIN, PPY, GLUCAGON, GONADOTROPIN-RELE...
RELEASING HORMONE, HUMAN CHORIONIC GONADOTROPIN, HUMAN PLA...
INHIBIN, INSULIN, INSULIN-LIKE GROWTH FACTOR, LEPTIN, LUTEINIZING HO...
HORMONE, OREXIN, OXYTOCIN, PARATHYROID HORMONE, PROLACTIN, REL...
AMYLIN, THROMBOPOIETIN, THYROID-STIMULATING HORMONE, THYROTROP...
CORTISOL DEHYDROEPIANDROSTERONE,   ALDOSTERONE, TESTO...
DIHYDROTESTOSTERONE, ESTRADIOLESTRONE, ESTRIOL, PROGEST...
CALCIFEROL, PROSTAGLANDINS, LEUKOTRIENES, PROSTACYCLIN, ...
HORMONE, LIPOTROPIN, BRAIN NATRIURETIC PEPTIDE, NEUR...
PANCREATIC POLYPEPTIDE, RENIN, ENKEPHALIN, OS...

Within her practice Tiffany adopts the role of a habitual observer, creating work that is a reflection of where she finds herself in relation to issues prevalent in the media or wider populace at any given time. As part of this process, she observes herself and people around her: How we carry our bodies, casual gestures and interactions, the exteriors we choose to present to others, and the way this is reported and positioned in the media. Once a particular topic of interest emerges, she spends time researching associated images and text representations in order to gain a better understanding of the subject and place the work within a historical, social and/or personal framework. During this research period, possible ideas and mental images of potential work start to emerge, followed by a process of experimenting to select the best materials and methods to make the envisaged works a reality.

1	3	4
2		5
		6

1 Incise
2011
Skin, temporary tattoo
345×490×35 mm
Photography: Tobias Titz

2 Nourish
2011
Skin, temporary tattoo
345×490×35 mm
Photography: Tobias Titz

3-5 Pages from artist's sketchbook including work-in-progress images of the piece, Grow

6 A glimpse of Tiffany Parbs' studio

Petra Zimmermann

Petra Zimmermann occupies a unique position among the emerging contemporary jewelry artists: She shares their exciting approach to the subject of jewelry and the quotable adoption of the pop culture label for defining the auteur jewelry concept. She succeeds, this time through historical reference. The artist draws on past encounters with costume jewelry from the previous century for her rings, bracelets, and brooches. Comprised of bright, colorful, synthetic forms, these objects receive a framework, in which their artificial appearance contrasts with the dusty splendor of the historic costume jewelry. Thus, beguiling pieces of jewelry emerge, which combine the present fascination for glamour with an element of progression, thereby referencing the costume jewelry as an essential component in the production and construction of glamour in the portrait photography of the Hollywood diva.

1 | 2
3

1 Bracelet, 2012 – 1
Antique handbag (alpaca), polymethyl methacrylate, garnets, lacquer
Photography: Georg Mayer

2 Bracelet, 2013 – 1
Antique handbag (alpaca), polymethyl methacrylate
Photography: Petra Zimmermann

3 Bracelet, 2013 – 2
Antique handbag (alpaca), polymethyl methacrylate
Photography: Petra Zimmermann

In her latest series of works, the artist uses mass media images of models, floral motifs, architecture, and design objects, which broaden her scope of cultural and social interpretations. In this way, behind the visual opulence of her work, she succeeds in handling relevant aesthetic and social themes in her pieces – relevant for a generation that no longer struggles against traditional conventions, but that negotiates much more in an increasingly complex environment, in the search for personal and historical coherence.

4 | 5
6 | 7

4-5 Bracelet, 2012 – 2
Antique handbag (alpaca), polymethyl methacrylate, coral and amethyst beads, gold leaf, blackened silver
Photography: Petra Zimmermann

6-7 Bracelet, 2013 – 3
Antique handbag (alpaca), polymethyl methacrylate, garnets, lacquer
Photography: Georg Mayer

1 | 2

1 Necklace, 2013 – 1
Polymethyl methacrylate, mirror, printing
ink, white gold leaf, labradorit beads,
blackened silver
Photography: Petra Zimmermann

2 Necklace, 2013 – 2
Historic beadwork, polymethyl
methacrylate, printing ink, gold leaf,
lacquer, acrylic color,
blackened silver, brass
Photography: Petra Zimmermann

3 Ring, 2013 – 1
Polymethyl methacrylate, labradorite beads, gold
Photography: Petra Zimmermann

4 Ring, 2013 – 2
Polymethyl methacrylate, costume jewelry findings, gold
Photography: Petra Zimmermann

5 Ring, 2010 – 3
Vintage costume jewelry, polymethyl methacrylate, lacquer, gold
Photography: Petra Zimmermann

1 Petra Zimmermann and her work
Photography: Wolfram Otto

2 Brooch, 2011 – 1
Polymethyl methacrylate, costume
jewelry findings, gold
Photography: Petra Zimmermann

3 Brooch, 2011 – 2
Polymethyl methacrylate, printing ink,
gold leaf, lacquer, acrylic color, crushed
pearls, amethyst, blackened silver
Photography: Petra Zimmermann

4 Jewelry on wearers
Photography: Petra Zimmermann

Zhang Xiaoyu

Nowadays we have become increasingly accustomed to greeting each other on the Internet, while face-to-face communication occurs less and less. Zhang Xiaoyu hopes that jewelry can serve as a medium to create chances for real communication.

Jewelry is not only a carrier of self-expression; what it transmits through the wearer should assist him or her to discover other possibilities in life, increase serendipities, and promote exchanges and communications among people. In order to enhance jewelry's function as a communicative carrier in the contemporary context, Zhang conducts exploration and experiments of new ways of how jewels convey information. Meanwhile, the advancement of technologies and materials have undoubtedly brought about new possibilities for jewelry design and enriched the ways of how jewelry transmits information. During her investigation into the expressiveness of jewels, Zhang infuses acoustic information into jewels in the form of sounds, which reinforces people's audio perception of jewelry. In order to further expand jewelry design, electronic sensing, and 3D printing technologies have become primary experimentation methods under the direction of interactive concepts. When the viewer is within forty-five centimeters of the wearer, the jewels will emit sounds through electronic sensors, which create new opportunities for communication.

1 45 cm – 1
2012
Composite materials, titanium steel, 925 silver, photosensitive resins, an electronic sensor, a loudspeaker
600×180×80 mm

Instruction:

◆ YVMIN
◇ 2012
◆ Jewelery

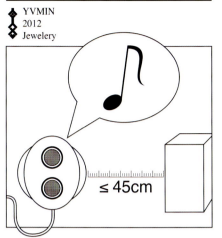

Ultrasound ①

③

②

④

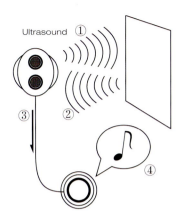

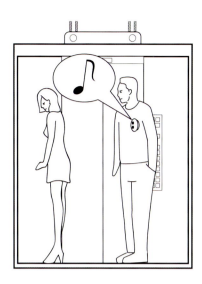

2 Users' guide

3 45 cm – 2
2012
Composite materials, titanium steel, 925 silver, photosensitive resins, an electronic sensor, a loudspeaker
1,700×80×60 mm

4 45 cm – 3
2012
Composite materials, titanium steel, 925 silver, photosensitive resins, an electronic sensor, a loudspeaker
160×120×50 mm

5 45 cm – 4
2012
Composite materials, titanium steel, 925 silver, photosensitive resins, an electronic sensor, a loudspeaker
200×60×50 mm

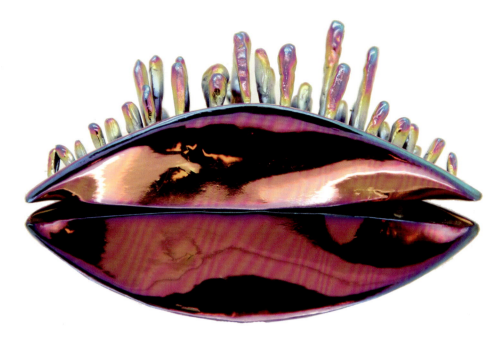

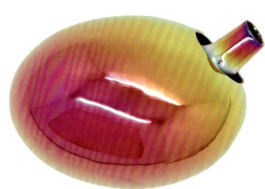

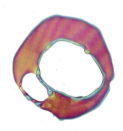

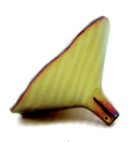

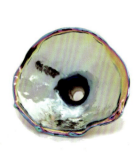

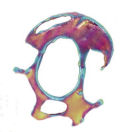

| 1 | 2 |
| | 3 |

1 Experiment with colors
2 Hand-painted drafts of inspirations
3 Pictures of creation process

Suska Mackert

Suska Mackert is a German jewelry artist who now serves as Dean of the Jewelry Design Department of Rietveld School of Art & Design Amsterdam. From 1988 to 1989, Suska studied philosophy, art history and play in Ludwig Maximilians University Munich, and learned glass and jewelry design in the State Vocational School for Glass and Jewelry and also in Rietveld School of Art & Design Amsterdam from 1989 to 1992. She has held many influential exhibitions across the world including "Properties" in Gallery Spectrum Munich in 2005; "Addenda & Errata" in Gallery Louise Smit Amsterdam in 2006; "An Order of Gloss" in Gallery Rob Koudijs Amsterdam in 2014. Her works have been collected by Rotasa Foundation, Stedelijk Museum Amsterdam, Jewelry Museum in Pforzheim and Museum of Art Craft in Itami. Her essays and interviews have been published in many professional publications.

As an artist, Suska Mackert reveals her thinking and research about jewelry art in her works. Most of her works are the artistic transference and manifestations of these inspirations. Since 1997, she has created few "practical" wearable jewels. On the contrary, she has become increasingly fascinated by the quality of jewelry as a phenomenon and the role it plays in our lives. During her probes into the significance of jewelry, she attempts to locate the boundaries of the concept of jewelry. She employs various media in her creations, which, apart from concrete jewels, also includes photos, videos, equipments, texts and print works. Instead of expressing the affection and favor of a certain jewel, she would prefer to view jewelry as a medium reflective of the entire cultural environment. Suska believes that jewelry should not be deemed as an isolated, self-sufficing field, rather, it should be seen as an indicator of the social psychology.

Although she doesn't create jewels according to their traditional forms and wearability, she doesn't totally discard them, either. Specifically speaking (take "Newspaper Collage" for instance), she observes closely how jewels or the wearers make their appearances in official and social activities. Worn by statesmen on political occasions, jewels and ornaments assert themselves in an ambiguous and vague identity. Suska extracts such images and occasions out for display and discusses the reflections of jewelry under certain contexts. What she pursues is not the creation of pieces of jewelry, but contemplation and experience of this world through jewelry.

1 | 2

1 Kette
Object, 2008
Paper
Diameter: approx. 200 mm
Photography: Suska Mackert

2 Rockstar / Kameltreiber
2011
Newspaper, DinA3 Scan

3 | 4   **3-4**   Newspaper Collage
5   **5**   The Diamond
                   Object, 2011
                   Paper
                   Diameter: 210 mm
                   Photography: Suska Mackert

EPILOGUE

Jewelry, as a cultural carrier, boasts an extended history as long as human history, spanning from the Paleolithic Era up to today. It is easy to capture humanitarian and cultural traits of an era through jewels of that time. They are the most minute yet most remarkable symbols of the development course of human history. Nowadays, with rapid advancements in technology and human civilization, artistic forms have become even more diversified, which finds full expression in the drastic transformations of shapes, materials, functions, and even significances of jewels. Contemporary jewelry art takes its place on this modern stage. Shrugging off traditional meanings such as showing off wealth, praying for blessings, bearers of inheritance, and symbols of privileges, contemporary work now aims at the exploration and research into the essence of jewelry – its relationship with human beings. In other words, contemporary jewels are no longer ornaments, but an artistic form, which mirrors mental acts such as emotions, philosophies, and thoughts.

Contemporary jewelry art, as a new form of art, has confronted doubts and misunderstandings whice arousing people's curiosity. This is quite common if perceived from the perspective of art history. For instance, drawings no longer assumed the role of recording facts when photography emerged, but shifted to the expression of emotions and notions. After the explorations of artists across the ages, various artistic forms diametrically different from traditional ones asserted themselves on the stage of art history, such as the Impressionism, Cubism, Dada, and Pop Art. Likewise, contemporary jewelry art is also the crystallization of constant exploration by jewelry artists. Although at present it is comparatively young, there is no doubt that it will find its brilliant niche in the history of art.

As a practitioner in the industry of contemporary jewelry art, I feel privileged and grateful for having received the invitation from CYPI Press to write and compile this book. Currently in the market, there are few readings with a professional perspective for the general public such as this one, which offers some unbelievable academic studies and collections of works. The publication of this book testifies to the fact that increasingly more people are following and getting to know the essence and spirit of this new art form, an optimistic sign that even more people will engage in the development of it and contribute to its further advancement through constant exploration. That is why this book endeavors to cover the full spectrum of contemporary jewelry art with selections of representative artists and works from all art divisions, coupled by the experiences and creations processes of many artists. This book will offer an eye-opener for readers to get into the vast world of contemporary jewelry art and cater to their aspirations for related knowledge.

At last, I would like to extend my sincere thanks to all staff members at CYPI Press for their industrious work, to every contemporary jewelry artist featured in this book for their full support, and to Professor Jivan Alstfalck and Professor Teng Fei for their patient guidance. We are firmly convinced that, with constant endeavors and explorations, contemporary jewelry art will shine brilliantly!

Li Puman

April 2014, Beijing

In 2008 she was awarded, among other distinctions, the City Goldsmith's Price in Hanau (DE). She was a lecturer at the Rietveld School of Art & Design from 2000 till 2008; currently, she is Director of the Jewelry Design Program at St. Lucas University College of Art & Design Antwerp (BE). Her work has featured in private and public collections, most notably in the CODA Museum, Apeldoorn (NL), the Design Museum, Ghent (BE), and the FNAC, Paris (FR).

Iris Eichenberg

Iris Eichenberg, Germany, b. 1965
From 1998 to 2000, Iris studied the Teacher Training Course at University of Amsterdam. In 2001, she was awarded Artist in Residence, European Ceramic Work Center (EKWC) in Hertogenbosch, NL; the Nomination Design Award, Museum Boijmans Van Beuningen, Rotterdam, NL and the Basic Grant, Fonds BKVB, Amsterdam, NL. In 2002, she was awarded the Incentive Grant, Fonds BKVB, Amsterdam, NL. In 2005, she was awarded the Incentive Grant, The Netherlands Foundation for Visual Arts, Design and Architecture (Fonds BKVB), Amsterdam, NL.

Jivan Astfalck

Jivan Astfalck, Germany, b. 1959
In 1982, Jivan Astfalck qualified as Goldsmith in Berlin Chamber of Handicrafts, Germany. In the year of 2007, she graduated from Chelsea College of Art and Design of the University of the Arts London, getting a PhD in Fine Art. From 1999 to 2004, she served as senior lecturer for BAs (Bachelor of Art) of Jewelry & Silversmithing in School of Jewelry of Birmingham Institute of Art and Design (BIAD) of Birmingham City University, UK.

Kazumi Nagano

Kazumi Nagano, Japan, b. 1946.
From 1970 to 1972, Kazumi Nagano earned her Master's in Art at Tama University of Art in Tokyo . In 1996, she began to study jewelry under Ms. Minato Nakamura. In 2002, she

was awarded the Fine Works Prize in the Japan Jewelry Art Competition, Tokyo.

Kim Buck

Kim Buck, Denmark, b. 1957
From 1983 to 1985, Kim studied at the Danish Institute of Precious Metal, specializing in Jewelry Design. From 1998 to 2000, he taught at HDK of University of Gothenburg. Since 2004, he has taught at Konstfack in Stockholm, Sweden as a professor.

Li Anqi

Li Anqi, China
Li Anqi graduated from China Central Academy of Fine Arts (CAFA) in 2012. She is pursuing her Master's Degree in Rhode Island School of Art and Design, USA. Her works were selected by Beijing Expo 2010 and Beijing International Jewelry Art Biennial.

Li Puman

Li Puman, China
Li Puman graduated from China Central Academy of Fine Arts (CAFA) with a major in Jewelry Arts in 2010. Since 2008, she has been a columnist for a magazine called "Trends Time." She joined the Gems & Jewelry Trade Association of China and China National Arts and Crafts Society in 2009. Her works earned the "New Crafts Exploration Award" granted jointly by CAFA and Hiersun in 2010. She also assisted in the curation for "10 Years – Re: Jewelry" Contemporary Jewelry Exhibition by CAFA in 2012 and the compilation of the catalogue of this event.

Liu Xiao

Liu Xiao, China
Liu Xiao obtained a Bachelor's Degree in Jewelry in 2008 and a Master's Degree in 2011, both from China Central Academy of Fine Arts (CAFA). His works have been exhibited in many countries and regions including Australia, the Netherlands, Germany, the UK, Spain, Japan, Thailand, and Taiwan. In 2012, he became the only Chinese artist who was selected for "Schmuck 2012"– the 64th

Contemporary Jewelry Exhibition in Munich. In 2013, he was awarded the Premi Joid'art– Enjoia't in Spain. Liu is a jewelry lecturer at CAFA.

Mari Ishikawa

Mari Ishikawa, Japan, b. 1964
Mari graduated from Nara University of Education in 1986 and worked in AIM Creator as an interior and graphic designer. She studied at the Academy of Fine Arts, Munich, in 1994 following Professor Otto Kunzli. She received successively the Germany Herbert Hoffman Prize, First Prize in the Bohmler Art Award, Second Prize in the Tahitian Pearl Trophy, the Advancement Award for Applied Arts 2009, Munich, and the Bavarian State Award 2010, Munich.

Märta Mattsson

Märta Mattsson, Sweden
Märta Mattsson majored in Jewelry Art at the School of Design and Crafts in HDK, Gothenburg, Sweden. She earned her Master's at the Royal College of Art, UK, in 2010. Märta has held many lectures across various countries. She won the First Prize in the Overall Excellence Award in London in 2010, and the Talent Prize in Munich, Germany in 2012.

Nanna Grønborg

Nanna Grønborg, Denmark, b. 1966
Nanna pursued Architecture Design in the University of Oregon, USA, from 1986 to 1987. In 1993, she won the Goldsmith Certificate and served as an assistant in professor Hermann Jünger's studio. In 1996 she earned a Master's Degree from the School of Jewelry, Birmingham City University, UK, and founded her own studio.

Petra Zimmermann

Petra Zimmermann, Austria, b. 1975
From 1996 to 1998, Petra studied in the Department of Jewelry and Metal at the Academy of Fine Arts and Design in Bratislava. And from 1997 to 2012, she pursued her

Master's Degree in Sculpture in the University of Applied Arts Vienna following professor Brigitte Kowanz. Petra won the Eligius Jewelry Award in Land Salzburg, Austria, in 2010 and the Contemporary Jewelry Award from the Cominelli Foundation of Italy in 2011. And in the following year, she opened a workshop and lecture, Jewelry Stories, in Konstfack, Stockhom, Sweden.

Rachel Darbourne

Rachel Darbourne, UK
Rachel Darbourne studied in Middlesex University, majoring in Jewelry Art, and later obtained a Master's Degree at the Birmingham School of Jewelry. After establishing her own workshop in 2008, Rachel served as an artist in residence at Birmingham School of Jewelry from 2013 to 2014. She was also an assistant curator for Suspended in Green.

Ramon Puig Cuyàs

Ramon Puig Cuyàs, Spain, b. 1953
From 1969 to 1974, Ramon Puig Cuyàs studied Jewelry Design at Escola Massana, Barcelona, Spain. Since 1997, he has been a professor of Jewelry Design and Head of the Jewelry Department in Escola Massana. Since 1988, he has been invited to numerous lectures and conferences at various schools, including the Royal College of Art, London; Copenhagen Technical College, Copenhagen; Estonia Academy of Arts, Tallin; Glasgow School of Art, Glasgow; Birmingham Institute of Art & Design, Birmingham; ESAD, Superior School of Art & Design, Porto; Nubre Project, Aswan, Egypt; Grey Area Gris Symposium, Mexico. In 1981, 1984, and 1994, he won the Herbert Hofmann Prize, I.H.M. in Munich, Germany.

Ruudt Peters

Ruudt Peters, the Netherlands, b. 1950
From 1970 to 1974, Ruudt studied at Rietveld Academy, Amsterdam. From 2004 to 2009, he was a professor in Adellab Konstfack

Stockholm SW. Since 2009, he has been a professor in Alchimya Contemporary Jewelry School in Florence, Italy. In 2004, he won the Herbert Hofmann Award, Munich, Germany.

Shen Yi

Shen Yi, China
Shen Yi graduated from China Central Academy of Fine Arts (CAFA) with a Bachelor's Degree in Jewelry Arts in 2007, and from Konstfack, University College of Arts, Crafts, and Design with a Master's Degree in Siversmithing and Jewelry in 2012. Her works were displayed at exhibitions such as "The State of Things," held in Munich Museum of Modern Arts, and "10 Years – Re: Jewelry" Contemporary Jewelry Exhibition by CAFA. Shen, now living in Amsterdam, is a co-founder of Goo Studio.

Sun Jie

Sun Jie, China
Sun Jie is a Chinese artist and founder of STUDIO JIESUN. He graduated from China Central Academy of Fine Arts (CAFA) in Beijing in 2007 and moved to Amsterdam, where he earned his Master's Degree from Rietveld School of Art & Design Amsterdam. In 2010, he founded his own studio, and won the Championship of Premi Joid'art-Enjoia't in Spain with his works collected in CODA Art Gallery, Holland. Meanwhile, he attended many important international design festivals and exhibitions over the years, such as 2009–2010 Art Rotterdam, 2010 Dutch Design Week, 2011 DMY International Design Festival Berlin, 2012 SOFA New York, 2012 Beijing Design Week, and 2012–2013 Collect London Design Week.

Suska Mackert

Suska Mackert, Germany, b. 1969
From 1998 to 2000, Suska studied at the Sandberg Institute, NL. Since 2004, she has studied in MA Studies at South Carelia Polytechnic in Lappeenranta, Finland, and joined Konstfack Workshop: object ID,

Stockholm. From 2007 to 2009, she taught in Rietveld School of Art & Design Amsterdam, NL. Since 2010, she has joined the Jewelry Department of the school.

Teng Fei

Teng Fei, China
Teng Fei graduated from China Central Academy of Fine Arts (CAFA) with a Bachelor's Degree in 1987, and from Berlin University of Art with a Master's Degree in 1995. She has been Head of the Jewelry Department in CAFA since 1995. Her works, "Chinese Box" and "Fables" won the Heinrich Bill Award in 1999, and her jewelry series, "Dialogue and Monologue," created in 2004, was awarded the Gold Prize at the 10th China National Fine Arts Exhibition.

Tiffany Parbs

Tiffany Parbs, Australia
Tiffany studied at the University of South Australia, Adelaide from 1989 to 1991, earning a Bachelor's Degree in Communication Studies. From 1994 to 1997 she pursued an Advanced Diploma in Applied and Visual Arts – Jewelry from the North Adelaide School of Arts in Adelaide, Australia. In 2003, after completing a mentorship under Susan Cohn, she worked as Assistant and Project Manager to Susan within Workshop 3000 in Melbourne, Australia. In 2007, Tiffany became an Artist in Residence at the School of Jewelry, Birmingham Institute of Art & Design, University of Central England. In 2011 she was awarded a Skills and Arts Development Grant by the Australia Council Visual Arts Board to undertake an Artist Studio Residency in London.

Wen-Hsien Hsu

Wen-Hsien Hsu, Taiwan, China
Wen-Hsien studied at Ming Chuan University in Taiwan, earning a Bachelor's Degree in Finance. In 2008, she studied Ornament Design at The European Institute of Design, Italy. From 2008 to 2011, she studied

contemporary jewelry in Alchimia following masters like Ruudt Peters and Peter Bauhuis. In 2013, she served as curator for exhibitions such as "Wear/Aware" New Asian Jewelry–"A jewelry a day keeps wrinkles away." and "More Than a Mother." Wen-Hsien is one of the founders of MANO Contemporary Jewelry & Object, an art jewelry gallery in Taipei.

Wu Junjin

Wu Junjin, China

Wu Junjin graduated from China Central Academy of Fine Arts (CAFA) in 2008 with a Master's Degree. One year before her graduation, she went to Glasgow School of Art in the UK as a visiting scholar. She now works as a lecturer in Hong Kong Design Institute. Wu won the Top Prize at the International Jewelry Design Awards 2006, and the Golden Prize of the Pearl Category at the CCTV (China Central Television) Jewelry Design Awards in 2007.

Wu Mian

Wu Mian, China

Wu Mian graduated from China Central Academy of Fine Arts (CAFA), majoring in Jewelry Arts in 2012 and now continues pursuing her Master's Degree there. Her work was exhibited at the 2011 International Metal Art Exhibition and won the Nomination Award by the President of CAFA. Her work was selected to exhibit at Galerie Marzee Annual International Graduation Show.

Yan Manjiang

Yan Manjiang, China

YanManjiang earned his Master's Degree from China Central Academy of Fine Arts (CAFA) with a major in Jewelry Arts in 2005. He has been a lecturer in Jewelry Design at CAFA since 2008. His work was listed on the 11th China National Fine Arts Exhibition, and "Pushing Boundaries & Chasing Challenges," the 2013 Beijing International Contemporary Metal Art Exhibition.

Yan Rui

Yan Rui, China

Yan Rui is the founder of an independent jewelry brand "Hard Candy." His works have won many awards from notable competitions, including Auditions China International Gold Jewelry Design Awards, HRD Awards International Diamond Jewelry Competition, and China Freshwater Pearl Jewelry Design Competition.

Yin Xiangkun

Yin Xiangkun, China

Yin Xiangkun graduated from China Central Academy of Fine Arts (CAFA) with a Bachelor's Degree in Jewelry Art. His works won the Third Prize of Graduation Works and Nomination Award by President of CAFA, and were selected by Beijing Expo 2012 and 2013 Sotheby's Exhibition, London. Yin is the founder of an independent designer jewelry brand "Essence."

Zhang Fan

Zhang Fan, China

Zhang Fan graduated from China Central Academy of Fine Arts (CAFA) with a major in Jewelry Arts in 2006, and thereafter became a lecturer at the Academy. Her works were listed on the 2009 International Metal Art Exhibition, and the 2010 Art Beijing Contemporary Art Fair. In 2012, she was praised by the French magazine *ELLE* as one of the twelve new leading ethnic Chinese designers around the globe. In 2013, her works were exhibited at Beijing International Jewelry Art Biennial.

Zhang Xiaoyu

Zhang Xiaoyu, China

Zhang graduated from China Central Academy of Fine Arts (CAFA), majoring in Jewelry Arts. Her work was exhibited at Galerie Marzee International Jewelry Exhibition, Holland, in 2012, and the 2013 Beijing International Jewelry Art Biennial. Zhang is the founder of the brand, YVMIN.

Contemporary Jewelry Design:
Thoughts on Inspiration and Expression

Authors: Liu Xiao, Li Puman
Commissioning Editors: Guo Guang, Mang Yu, Yvonne Zhao, Grace Feng
English Editors: Vera Pan, Jenny Qiu
Translator: Ling Yan
Copy Editor: Frances Moxley Zinder
Book Designers: Tang Tang, Sun Sujin

First published in the United Kingdom in 2014 by CYPI PRESS

Add: 79 College Road, Harrow Middlesex, HA1 1BD, UK
Tel: +44(0)20 3178 7279
Fax: +44(0)19 2345 0465
E-mail: sales@cypi.net editor@cypi.net
Website: www.cypi.co.uk
ISBN: 978-1-908175-48-9

Printed in China